Hanon Complete

The Virtuoso Pianist
In Sixty Exercises
For the Piano

T0078911

THE WILLIS MUSIC COMPANY

HANON ✗ THE VIRTUOSO-PIANIST

Preface

The study of the piano is today so general, and good pianists are so numerous, that mediocrity on this instrument is no longer endured. Therefore one must study the piano eight or ten years before venturing to perform a piece of any difficulty, even before amateurs.

Few persons can devote so many years to this study! So it often happens that for want of sufficient practice the playing is uneven and incorrect. The left hand fails in passages of slight difficulty; the fourth and fifth fingers are almost useless through lack of special exercises for these fingers, always weaker than the rest; and passages in octaves, in tremolo or trills are usually executed only with exertion and fatigue, a performance very incorrect and wholly wanting in expression.

The author has labored to overcome this state of affairs, trying to unite in one work special·exercises which render possible a complete course of pianistic study in much less time.

To attain this end, it sufficed to find the solution of the following problem:

If each of the five fingers of the hand were equally well trained, they all would be ready to execute anything written for the instrument, and the question remaining would be that of fingering, readily solved.

The author has found the solution of this problem in this book. Here will be found exercises necessary for the acquirement of agility, independence, strength and perfect evenness in the fingers, as well as suppleness of the wrists— all indispensable qualities for fine execution; furthermore, these exercises are planned to render the left hand equally skillful with the right. Excepting a few exercises to be found in several methods, the entire book is personal work. These exercises are interesting, and do not fatigue the student like the most of five-finger exercises, which are so dry that one needs the perseverance of a true artist to study them.

W. M. Co. 8214

Preface *Continued*

These exercises are written in such a manner that, after having read them a few times, they can be played quite rapidly; they are thus excellent practice for the fingers, and one loses no time in studying them. If desired, any of these exercises may be played on several pianos at the same time, rousing a spirit of emulation among the students, and habituating them to ensemble-playing.

All sorts of difficulties will be met with. The exercises are so arranged, that in each number the fingers are rested from the preceding. The result of this is, that all mechanical difficulties are executed without effort; and, with such practice, the fingers acquire astonishing facility of execution.

This work is for all piano-pupils. It may be taken up after the pupil has studied about a year. As for more advanced students, they will study it a very short time, and thereafter will never experience the stiffness previously felt in fingers or wrists; this will render them capable of surmounting the principal mechanical difficulties.

Pianists and teachers who have not time for sufficient practice, need only to play these exercises a few hours in order to regain all the dexterity of their fingers.

This entire volume can be played through in an hour; and if, after it has been thoroughly mastered, it be repeated daily for a time, difficulties will disappear as if by enchantment, and that beautiful, clear, clean execution will have been acquired. This is the secret of distinguished artists.

Finally, this work is offered as giving the key to all mechanical difficulties. Therefore it is considered that a real service is rendered to young pianists, to teachers, and to the directors of boarding-schools, in proposing their adoption of this work, "The Virtuoso-Pianist."

W. M. Co. 8214

The Virtuoso-Pianist
Part I
Preparatory Exercises for the Acquirement of Agility, Independence, Strength and Perfect Evenness in the Fingers

Extension between the fifth and fourth fingers of the left hand in ascending, and the fifth and fourth fingers of the right hand descending.

Studying the **20** exercises in this First Part, begin with the metronome at **60**, gradually increasing the speed up to **108**; the meaning of the double metronome-mark at the head of each exercise.

Lift the fingers high, strike with precision, playing each note very distinctly.

C. L. HANON

For brevity, we shall indicate only by numbers those fingers which are to be especially trained in each exercise; as, 3-4 in N⁰ 2; 2-3-4 in N⁰ 3, etc.

Notice that, through the book, both hands are continually executing the same difficulties. In this way the left hand becomes as skilful as the right. Also the difficulties executed by the left hand in ascending, are exactly copied by the same fingers of the right hand in descending. This new style of exercise will cause the hands perfect equality.

W. M. Co. 8214

As soon as Ex. 1 is mastered, go to Ex. 2 without stopping on this note

(3-4) When this exercise is mastered, repeat number one and play both together four times without interruption; the fingers will gain considerably by practising these exercises, and the following, in this way.

(1) The fourth and fifth fingers being naturally weak, it should be observed that this exercise, and the following to Nº 31, are intended to render them as strong and agile as the second and third fingers.

W. M. Co. 8214

4

(2-3-4) In beginning № 3, play the preceding exercises once or twice without stopping. When №3 is
mastered, practise № 4, and then № 5, and when they are thoroughly learned, play all four times
without interruption, not stopping until the last note on page 6. The entire work should be practiced
in this manner. So, when playing the numbers in the First Part, stop only on the last note on pp.
3, 6, 9, 12, 15, 18, and 21.

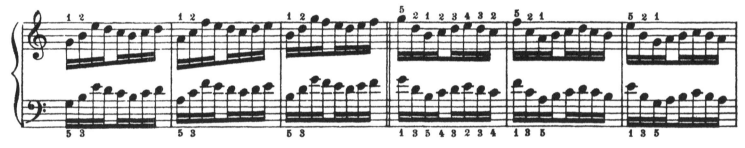

(3-4-5)(1)Special exercise for the 3rd, 4th and 5th fingers of the left hand.

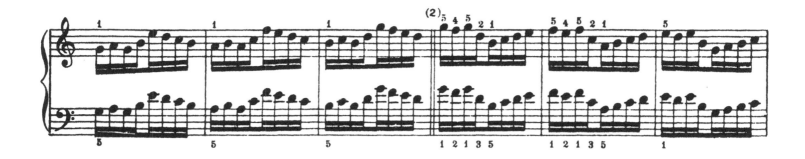

(2) Special exercise for the 4th and 5th fingers of the right hand.

W. M. Co. 8214

(1-2-3-4-5) We repeat, that the fingers be lifted high, with precision, until this entire volume is mastered.

(1) Preparation for the trill with the 4th and 5th fingers of the right hand.

W. M. Co. 8214

To obtain the good results which we promise those who study this work, it is indispensable to play daily, at least once, the exercises already learned.

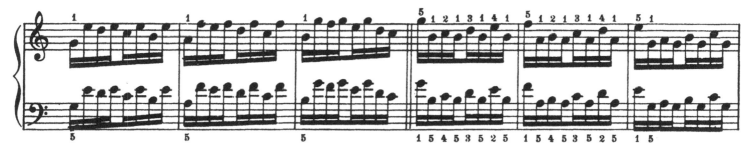

W. M. Co. 8214

(3-4-5) Exercise of the greatest importance for the 3rd, 4th and 5th fingers.

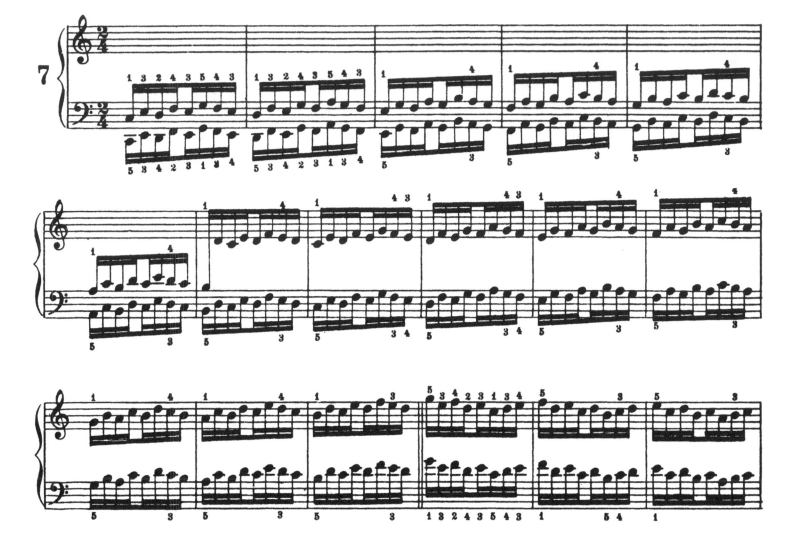

(1-2-3-4-5) Very important exercise for all five fingers.

W. M. Co. 8214

Extension of the 4th and 5th, and general exercise.

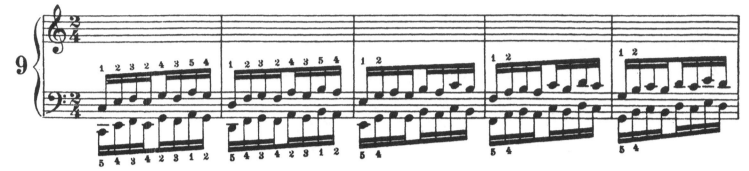

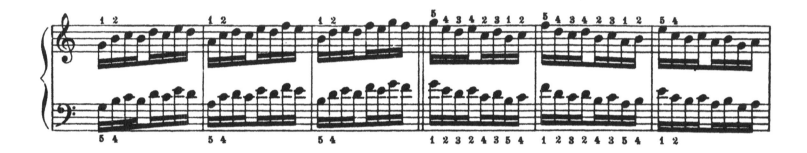

W. M. Co. 8214

(3-4) Preparation for the trill, for the **3rd** and **4th** fingers of the left hand in ascending **(1)**; and for the **3rd** and **4th** of the right, descending **(2)**.

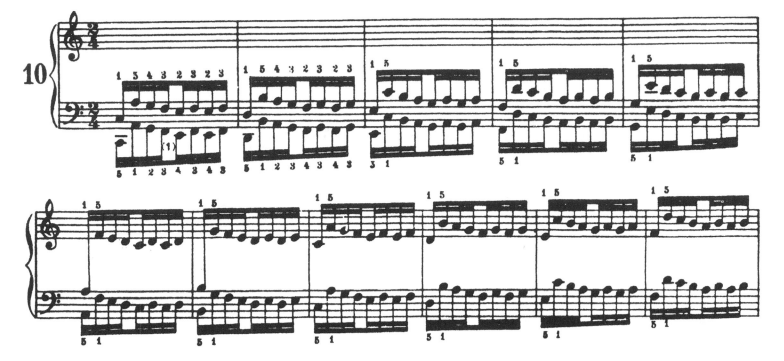

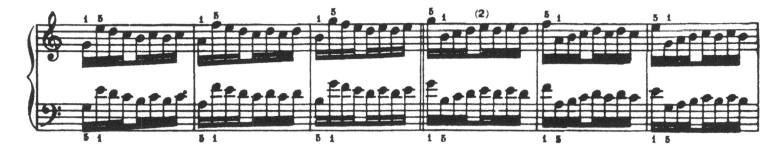

(3-4-5) Additional preparation for the trill, for the **4th** and **5th** fingers.

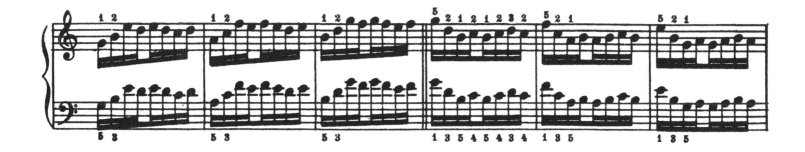

Extension of **1-5**, and exercise for **3-4-5**.

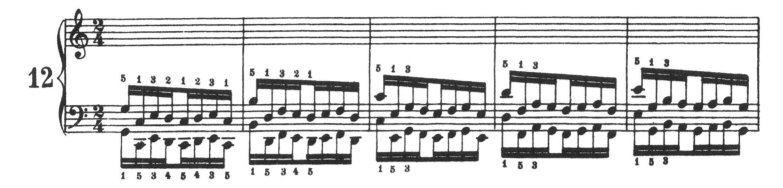

(3-4-5)

13

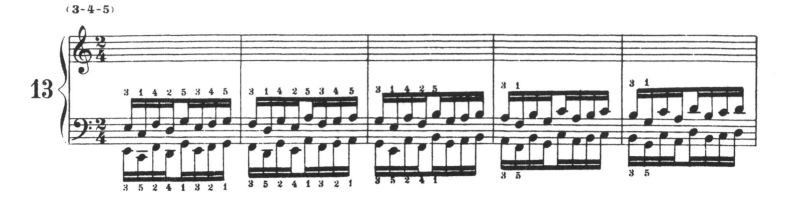

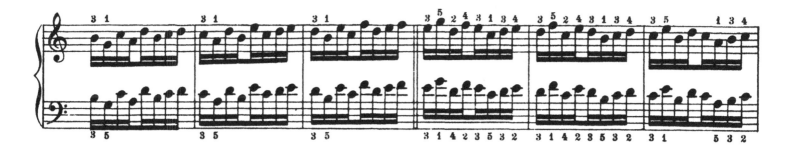

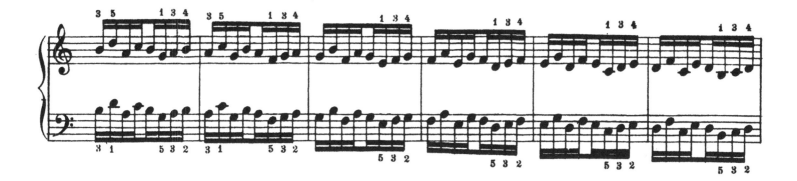

(3-4) Additional preparation for the trill, for the **3rd** and **4th** fingers.

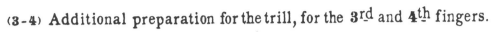

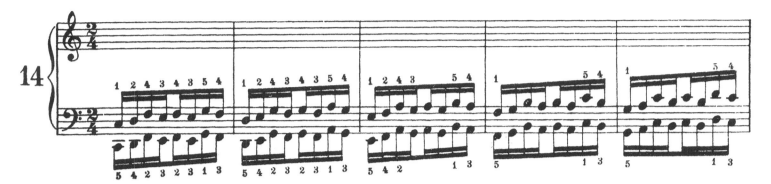

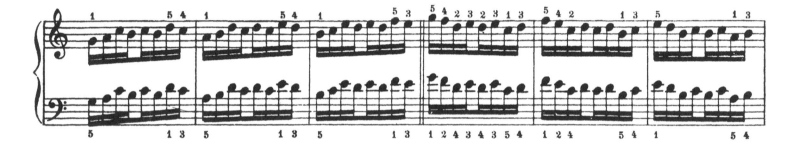

W. M. Co. 8214

Extension of **1-2**, and exercise for all five fingers.

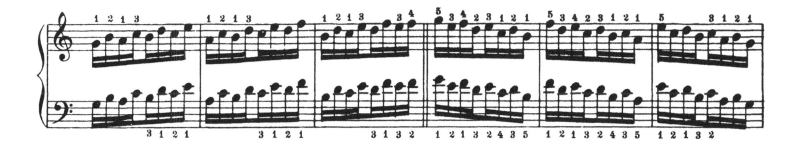

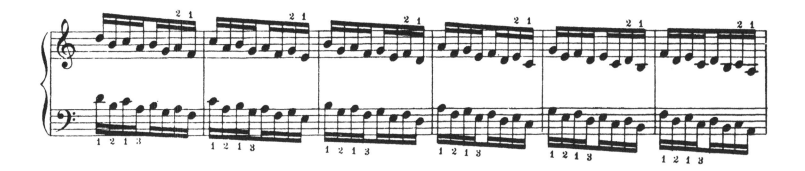

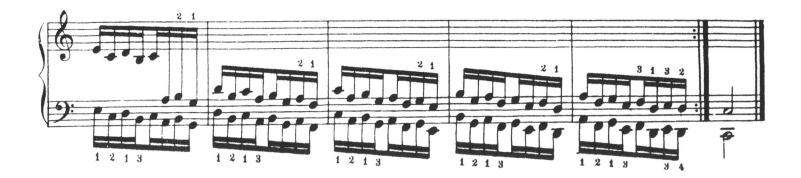

Extension of **3-5**, and exercise for **3-4-5**

16

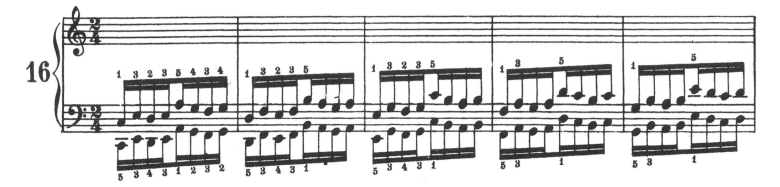

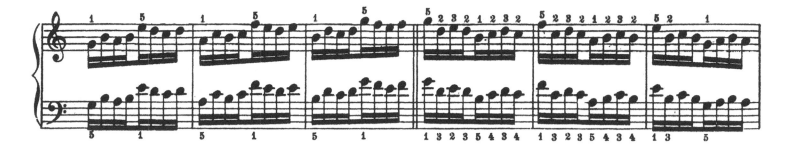

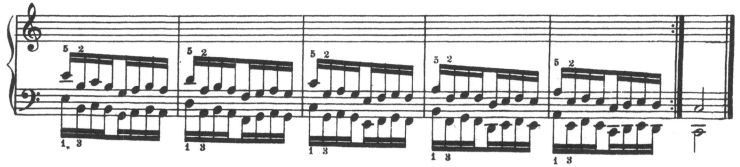

W. M. Co. 8214

Extension of 1-2, 2-4, 4-5, and exercise for 3-4-5.

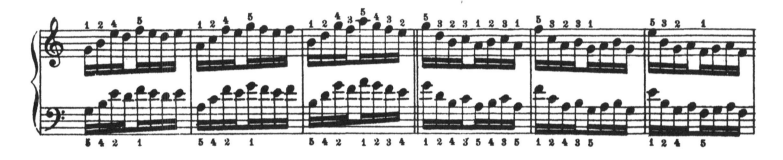

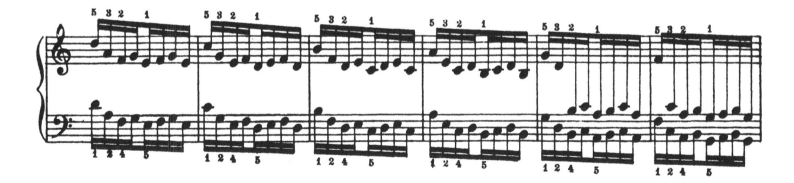

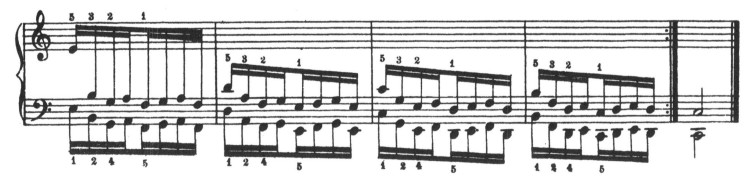

(1-2-3-4-5)

18

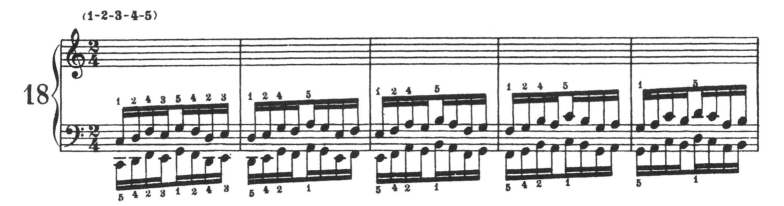

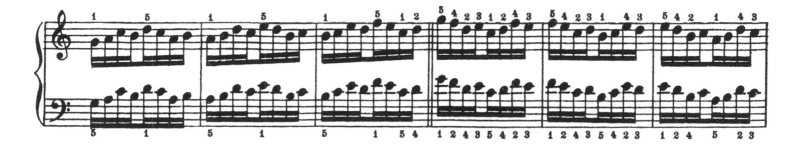

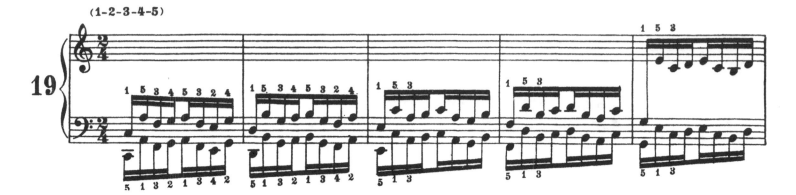

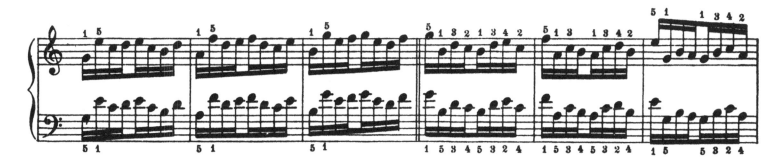

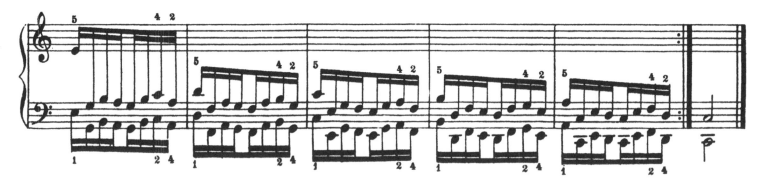

Extension of **2-4, 4-5**, and exercise for **2-3-4**.

20

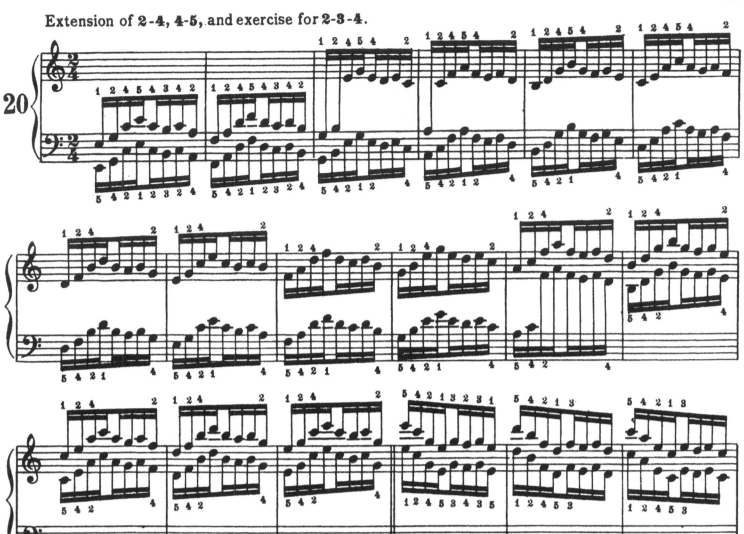

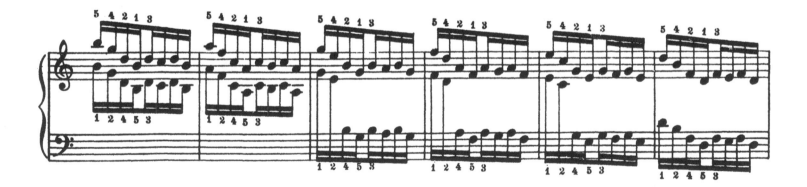

End of Part I.

After having learned this First Part, play it through once or twice daily before commencing the study of the Second ("transcendent") Part. One is sure to obtain every possible advantage that this work promises. Complete mastery of Part I gives the key to the difficulties found in Part II.

W. M. Co. 8214

Part II
Transcendent Exercises for Preparing the Fingers
for the Virtuoso Exercises:

Observe, that the work done by the 3rd, 4th, and 5th fingers of the left hand in the first half of each measure (A) is repeated inversely by the same fingers of the right hand in the last half of the same measure (B).

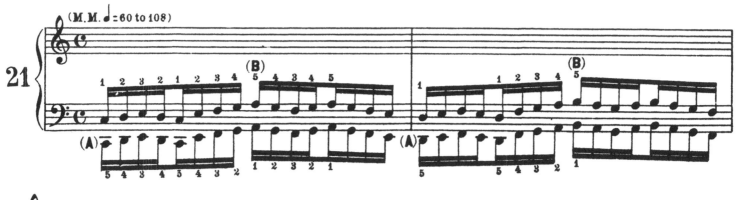

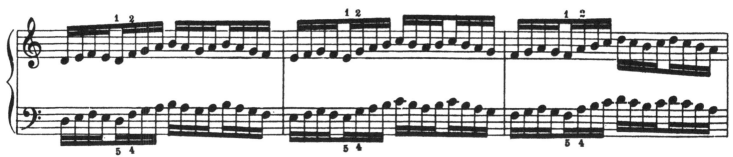

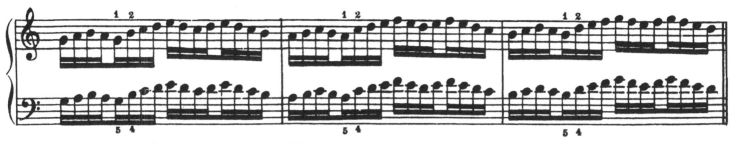

Practice the exercises in Part II, as in Part I, with the metronome at 60; and gradually increase the speed to 108. Wherever a different tempo is required it will be indicated at the head of the exercise.

W. M. Co. 8214

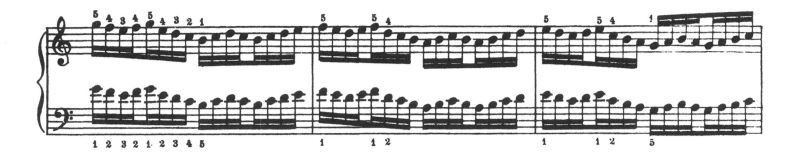

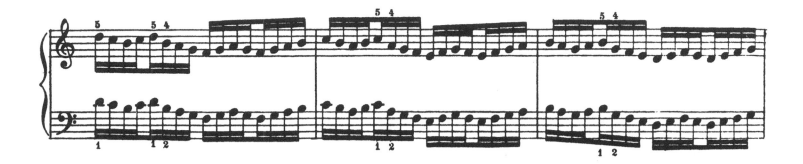

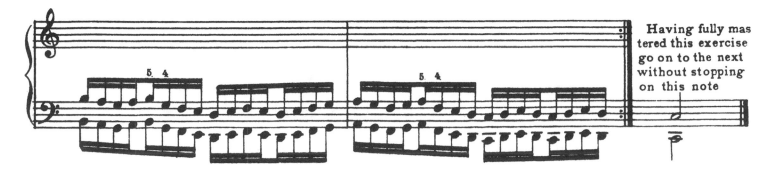

Having fully mastered this exercise go on to the next without stopping on this note

Same object as № 21. (3-4-5)

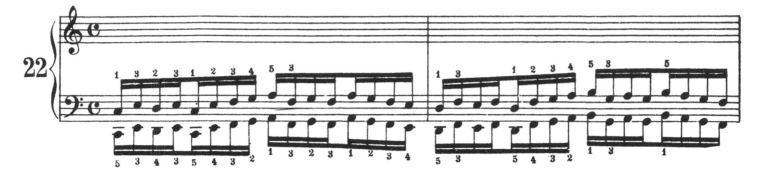

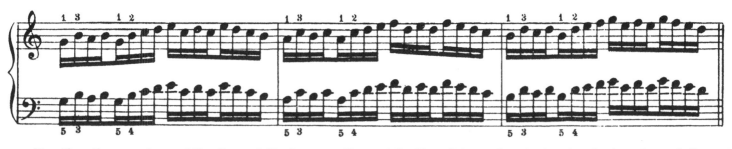

Practice the exercises of the Second Part as we directed for Part I (top of p. 4); thus, in playing through the exercises, stop only on the last notes on pp. 24, 29, 33, 37, 41, 44, 46, and 49.

W. M. Co. 8214

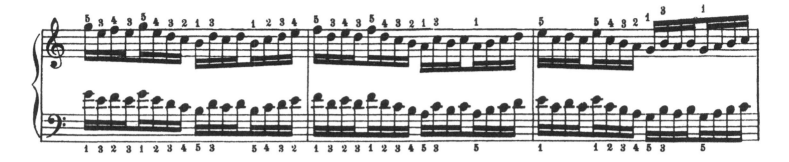

(3-4-5)

23

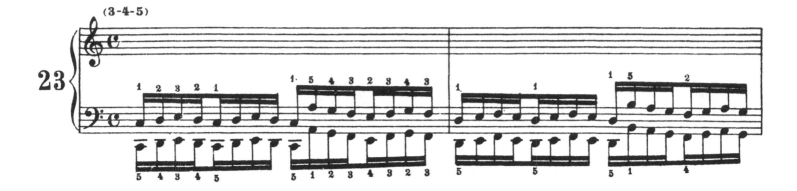

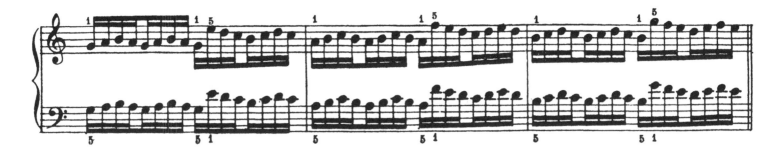

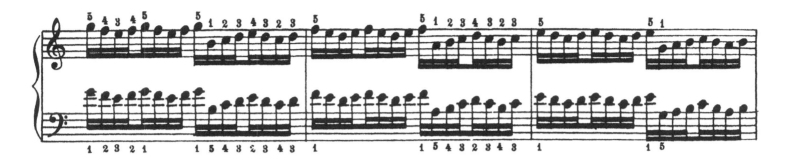

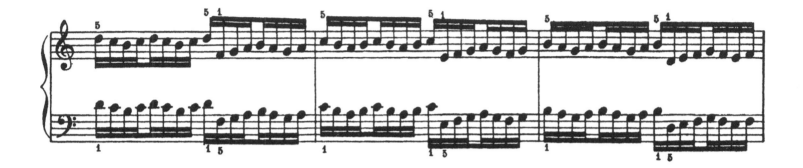

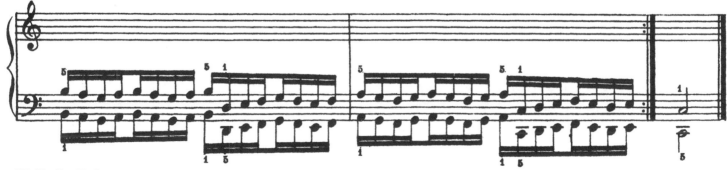

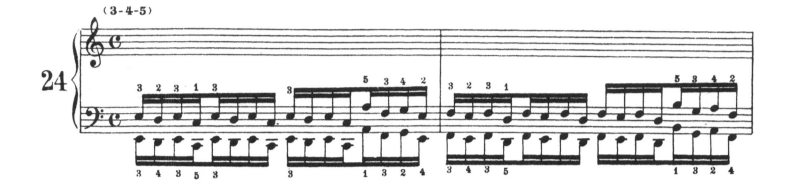

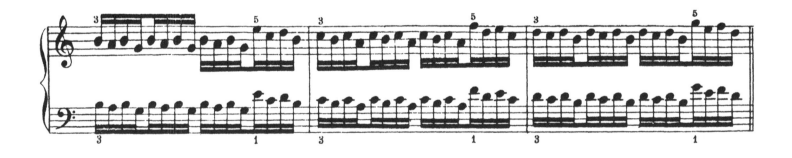

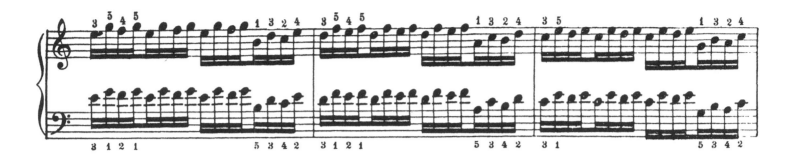

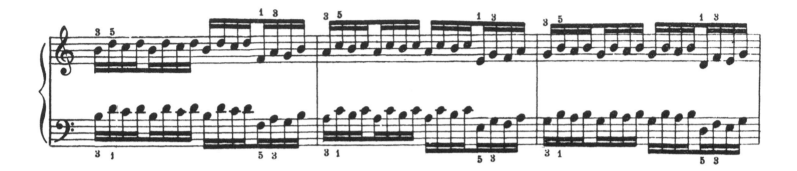

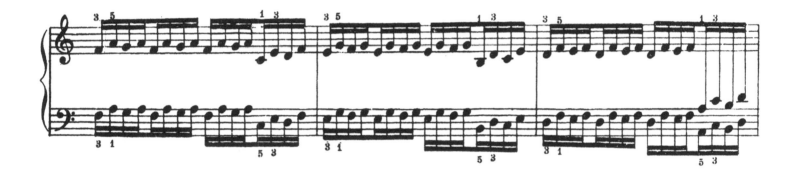

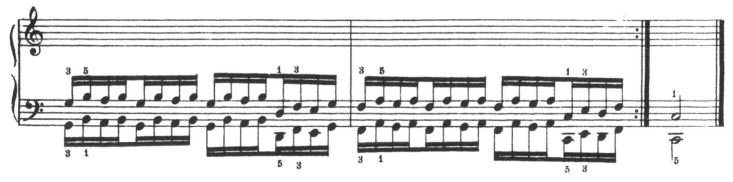

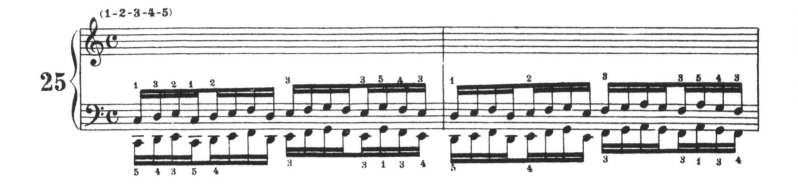

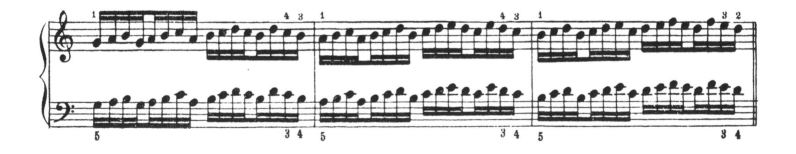

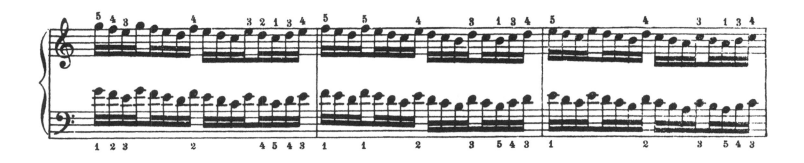

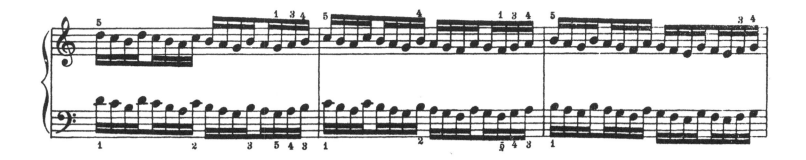

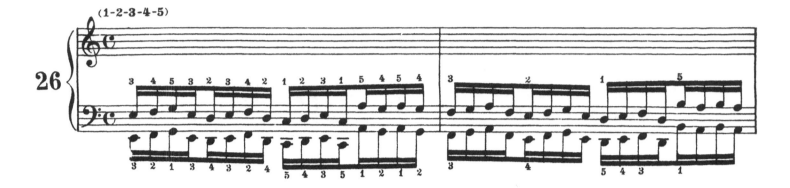

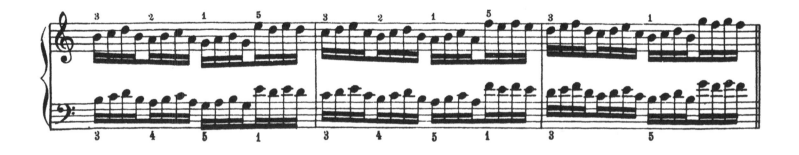

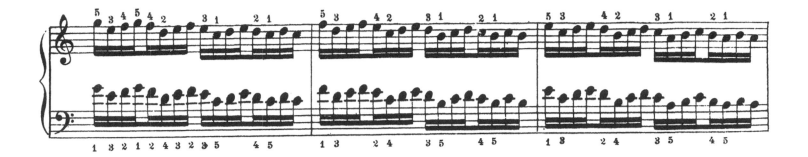

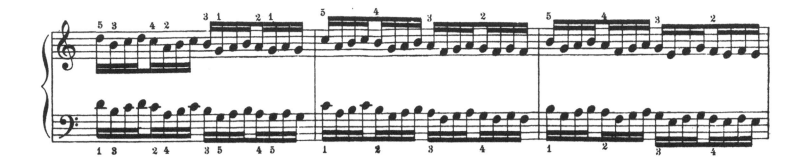

W. M. Co. 8214

34

(1-2-3-4-5) These prepare the 4th and 5th fingers for the trill given further on.

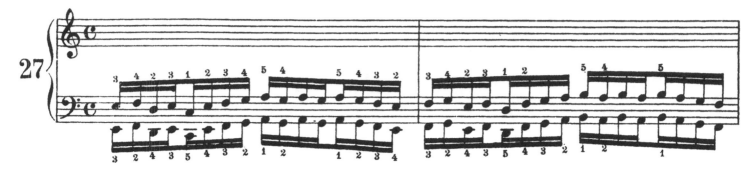

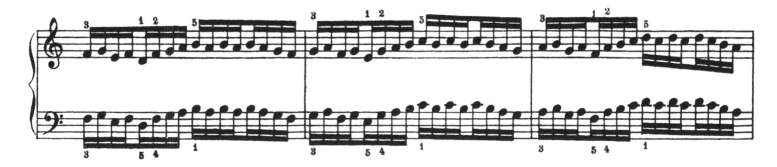

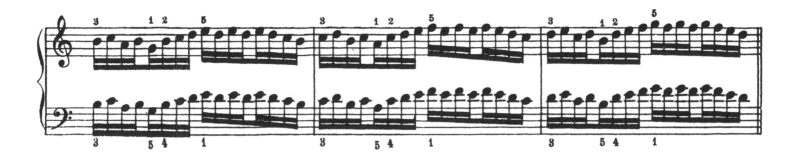

W. M. Co. 8214

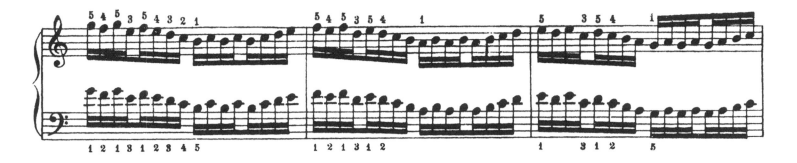

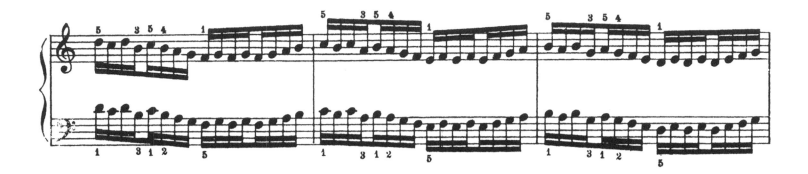

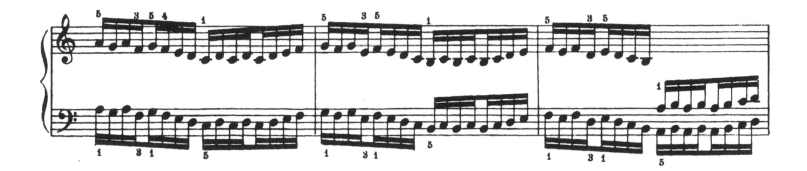

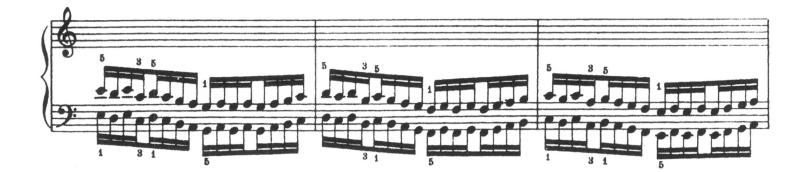

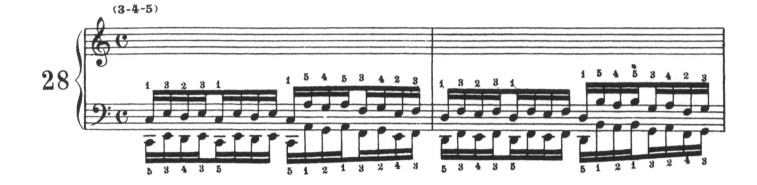

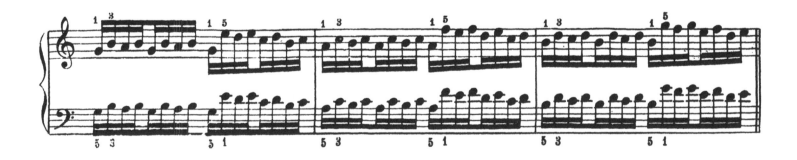

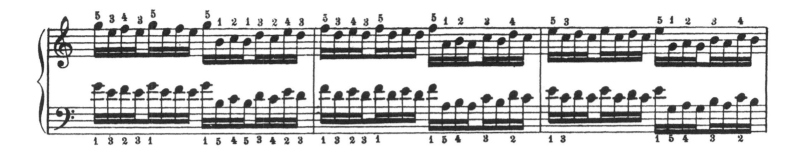

(1-2-3-4-5) Preparation for the trill, for all five fingers.

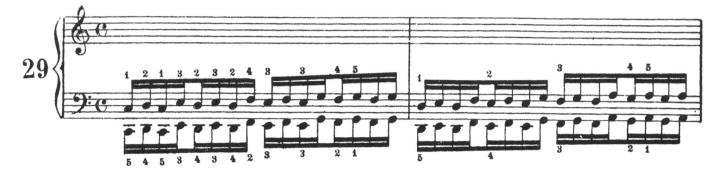

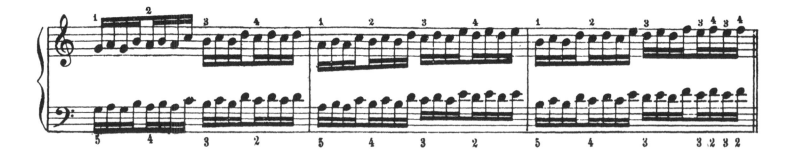

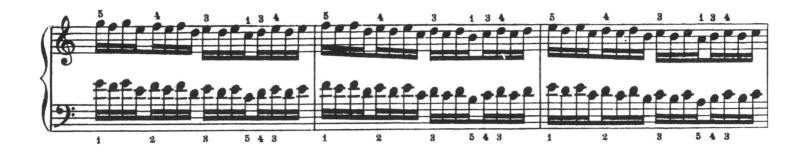

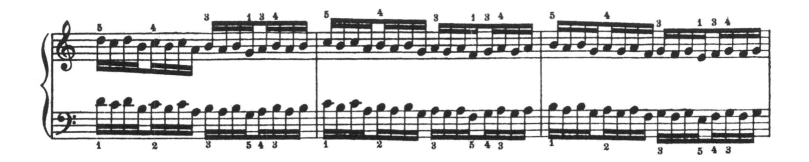

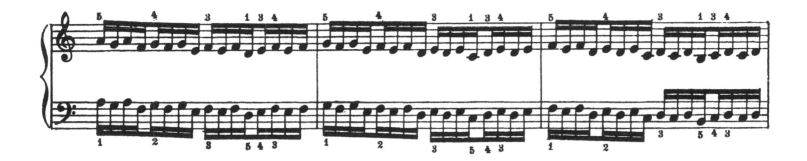

Trill alternating between **1-2** and **4-5**.

30

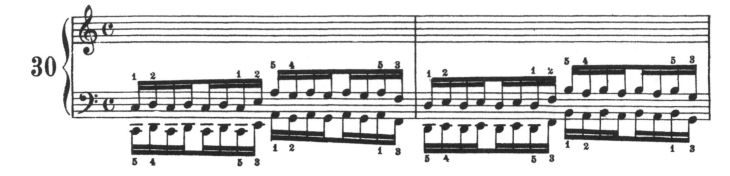

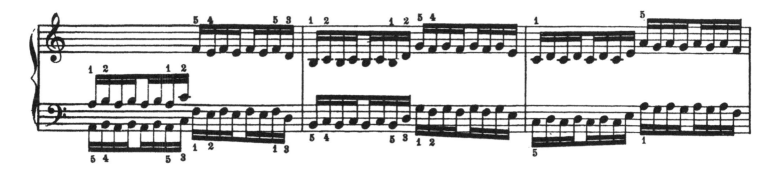

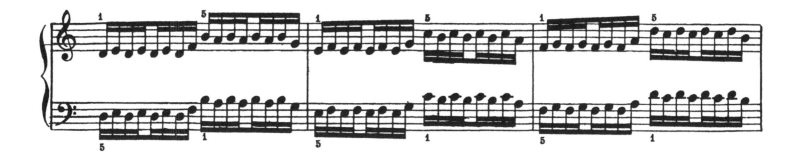

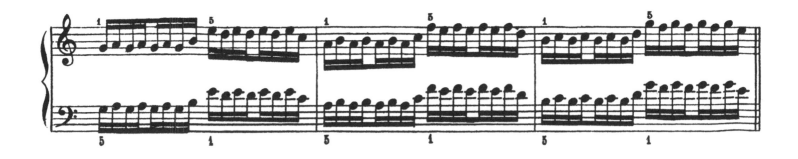

W. M. Co. 8214

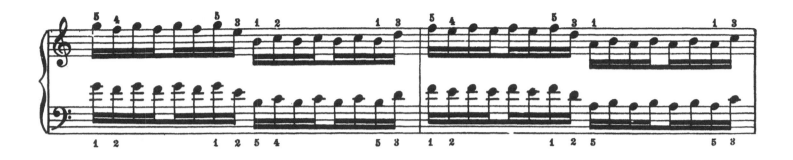

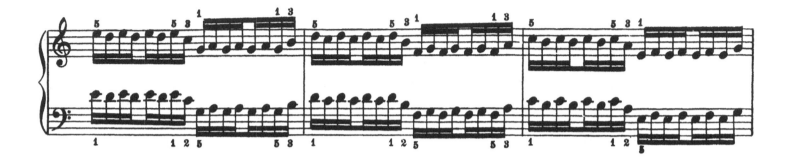

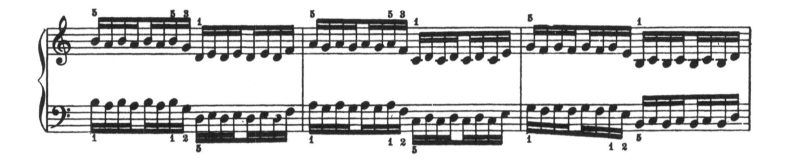

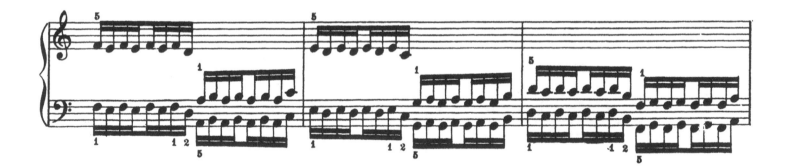

(1-2-3-4-5, and extensions)

31

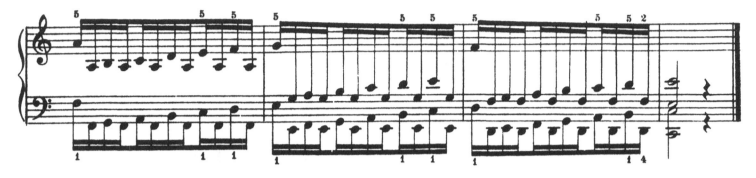

Thumb under

Turning the thumb under the 2d finger

M. M. ♩ = 40 to 72

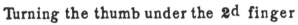

32

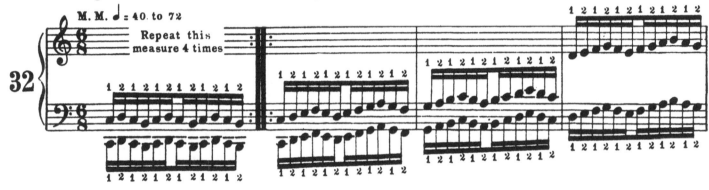

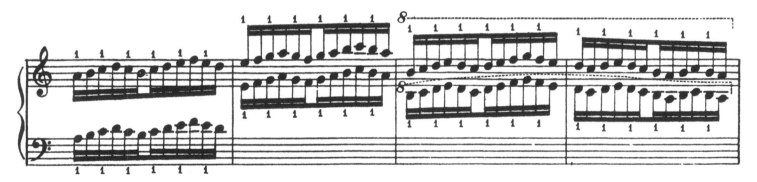

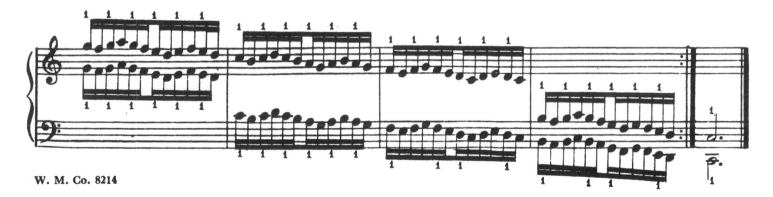

Thumb under the **3**d finger

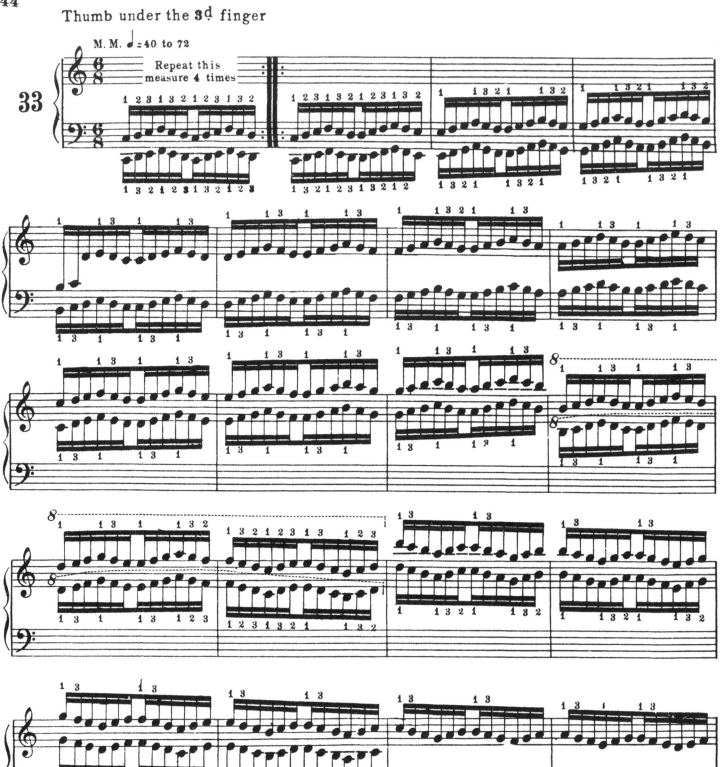

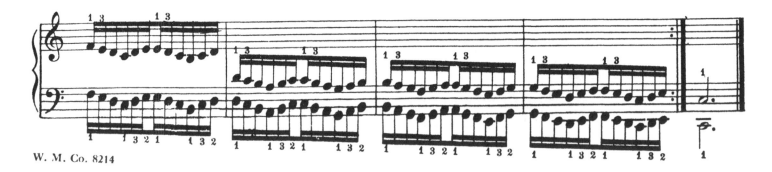

Thumb under the 4th finger

M.M. ♩ = 60 = 108

Repeat this measure 10 times.

34

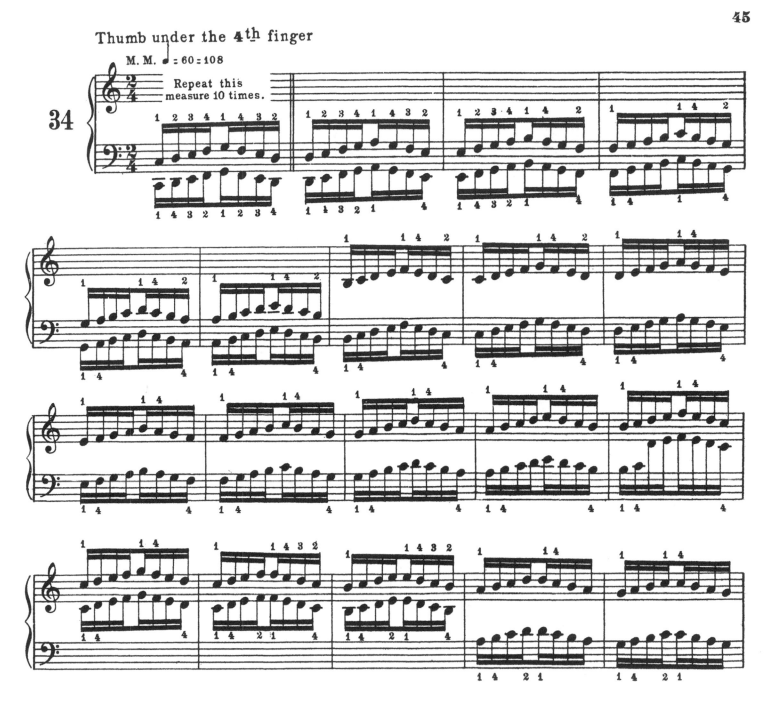

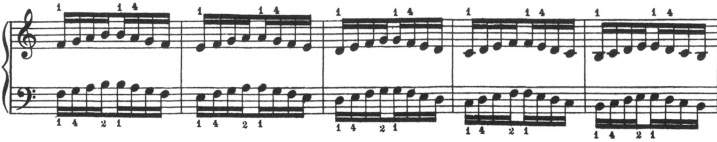

Thumb under the 5th finger. An exercise of the highest importance

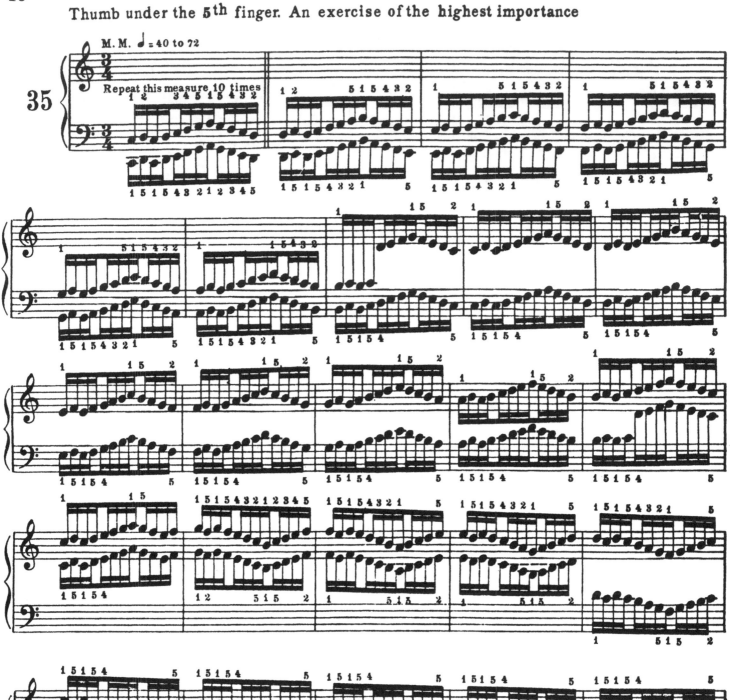

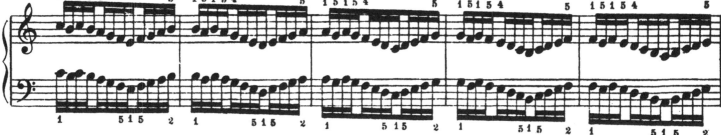

W. M. Co. 8214

Another example of the thumb under

Special exercise for the thumb under

Play this whole exercise with the thumbs only.

(1) Hold down these three notes with each hand without striking them, while executing these 12 measures

W. M. Co. 8214

Preparatory exercise for the study of scales

38

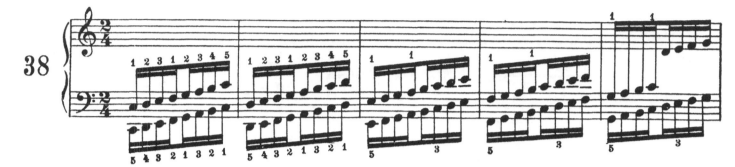

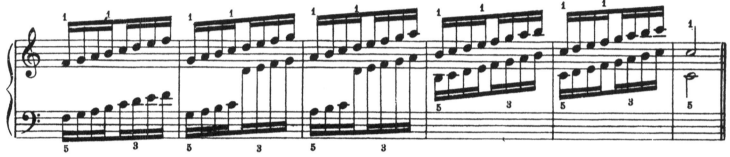

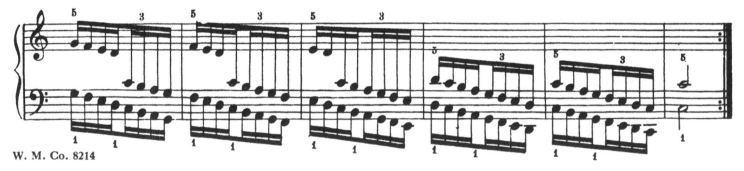

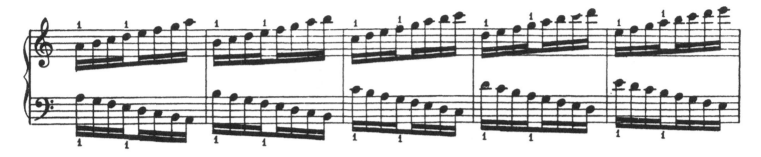

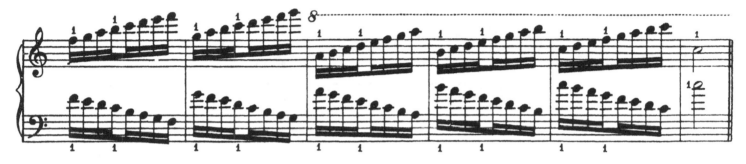

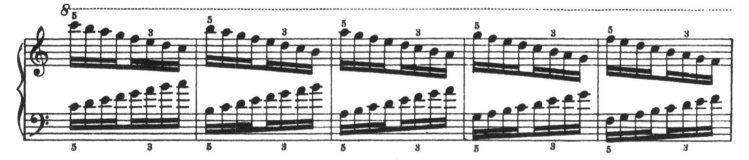

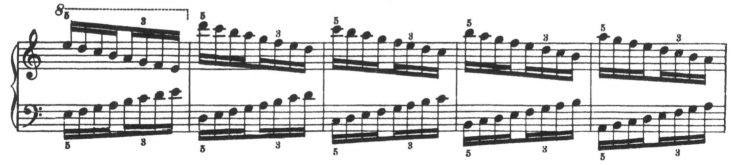

W. M. Co. 8214

The 12 Major Scales, and the 12 Minor Scales

Each major scale is followed by its relative minor

There are two ways of playing the minor scale. We think it best to give them here after each major scale, leaving it to the instructor to teach them as he pleases. We mark by figure **1** the first (modern) minor scale, also termed the "harmonic minor scale," and by a figure **2** the second (ancient) minor scale, also termed the "melodic minor scale."

We know, that the modern or harmonic minor scale has a minor sixth and the leading-note both ascending and descending; whereas the ancient or melodic minor scale has a major sixth and the leading note in ascending, and a minor seventh and minor sixth in descending.

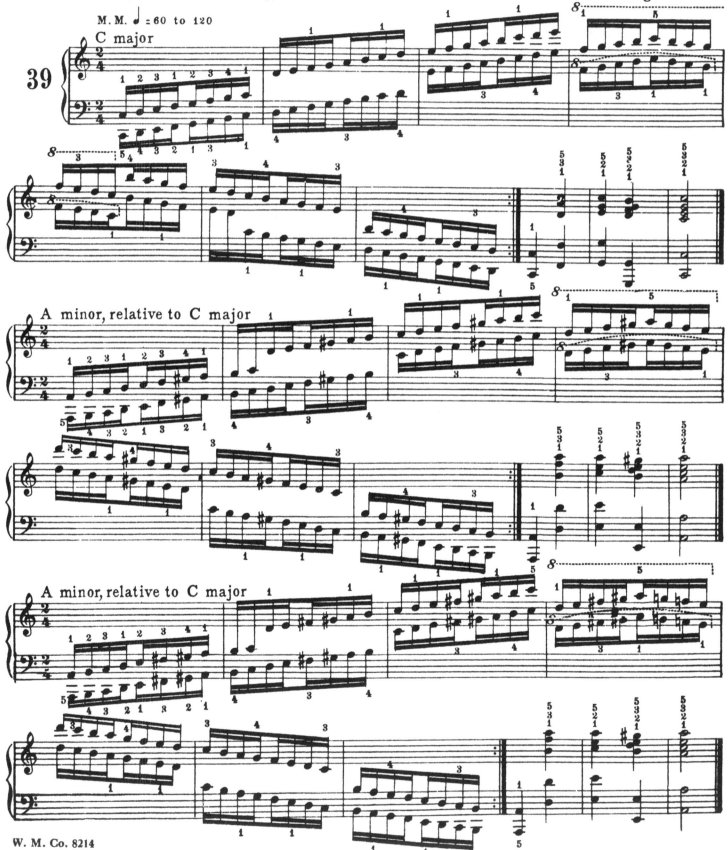

F major

1. D minor

2. D minor

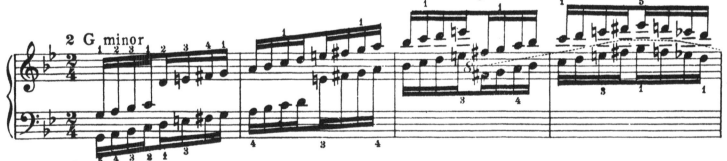

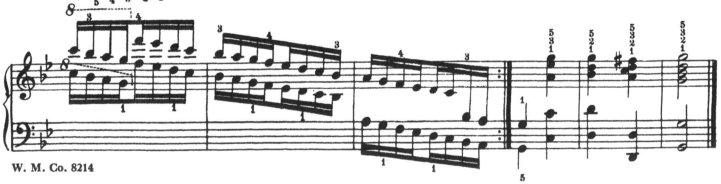

Eb major

1. C minor

2. C minor

Ab major

1. F minor

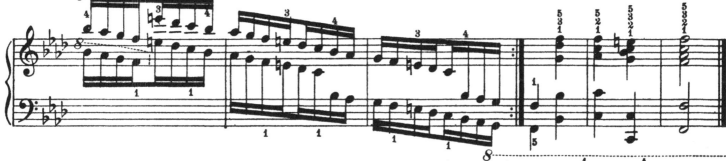

2. F minor

Db major

1. Bb minor

2. Bb minor

W. M. Co. 8214

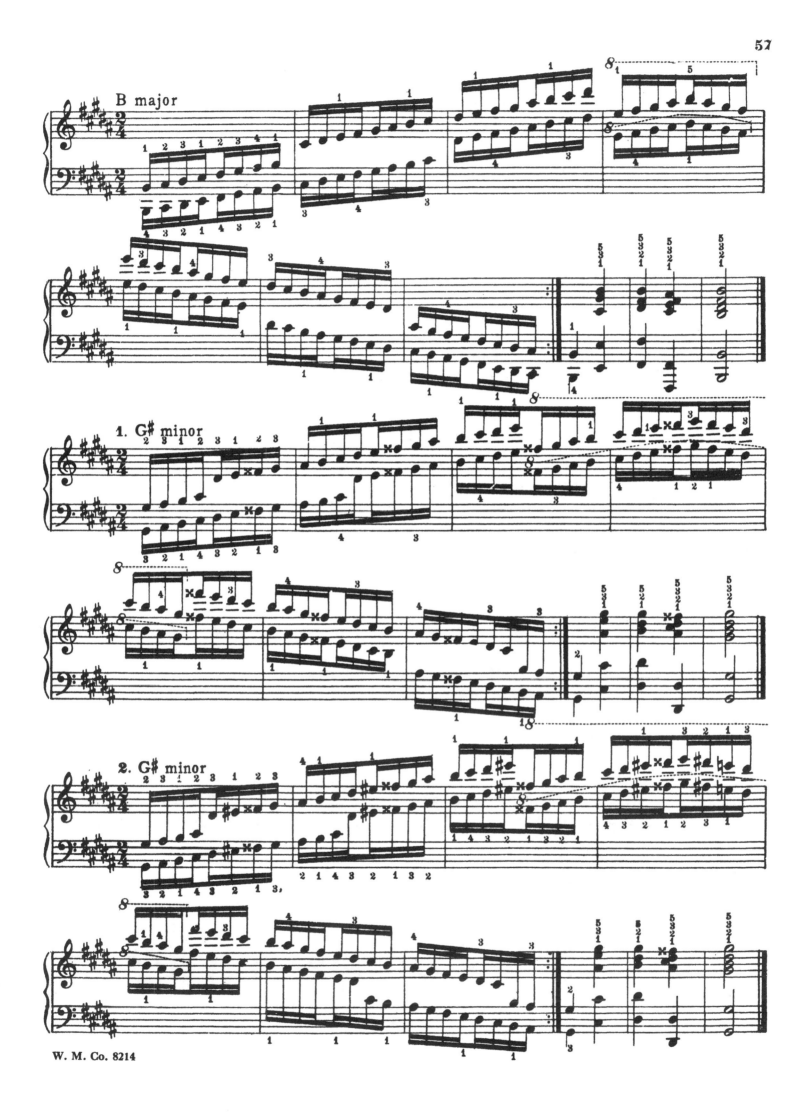

B major

1. G# minor

2. G# minor

58

A major

1. F# minor

2. F# minor

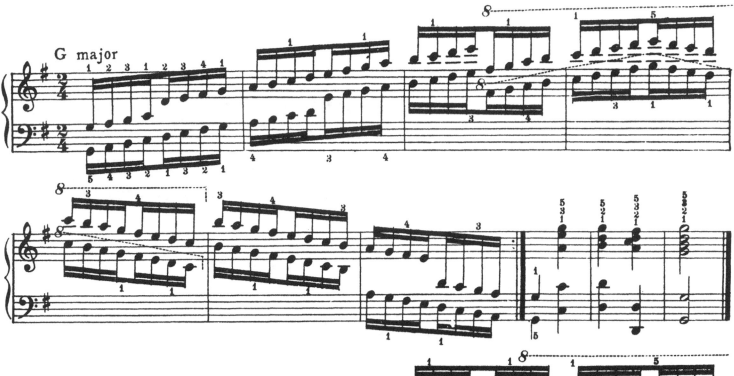

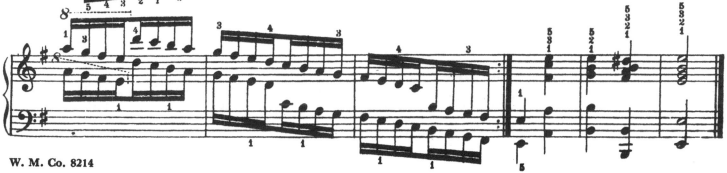

Chromatic Scales

(M. M. ♩ = 60 to 120)
At an octave

At a minor third

At a major sixth

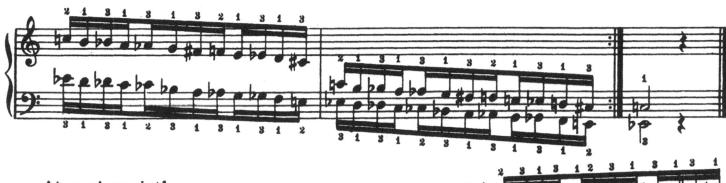

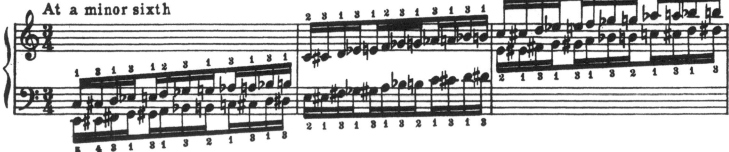

At a minor sixth

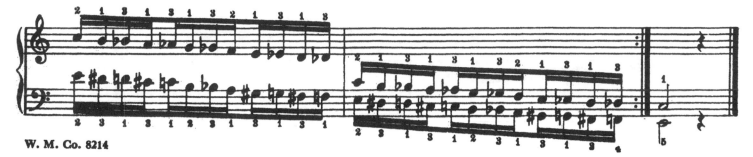

63

W. M. Co. 8214

64

In contrary motion, beginning on the octave.

In contrary motion, beginning on the minor third.

In contrary motion, beginning on the major third.

Another fingering, particularly recommended
for legato passages

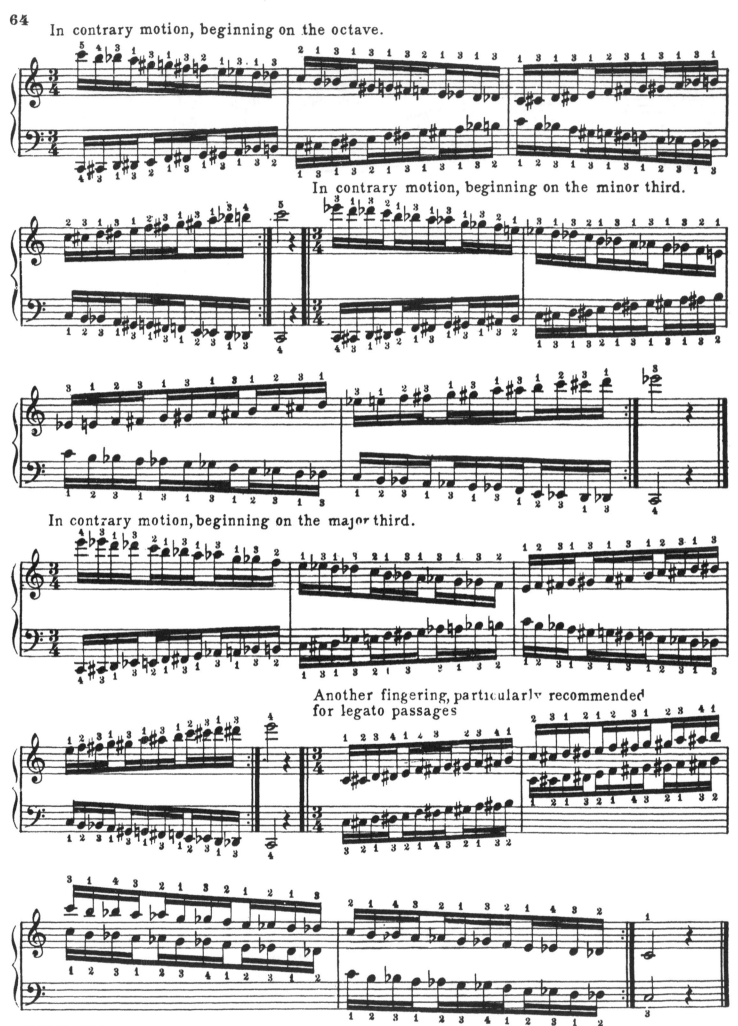

W. M. Co. 8214

Arpeggios on the Triads, in the 24 Keys

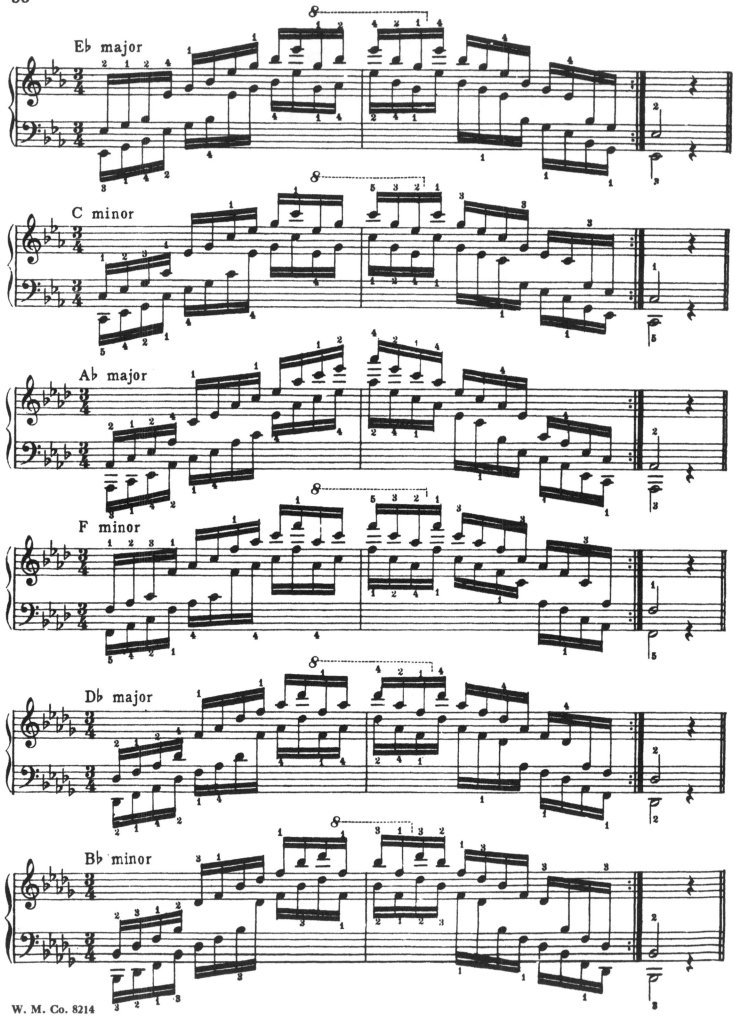

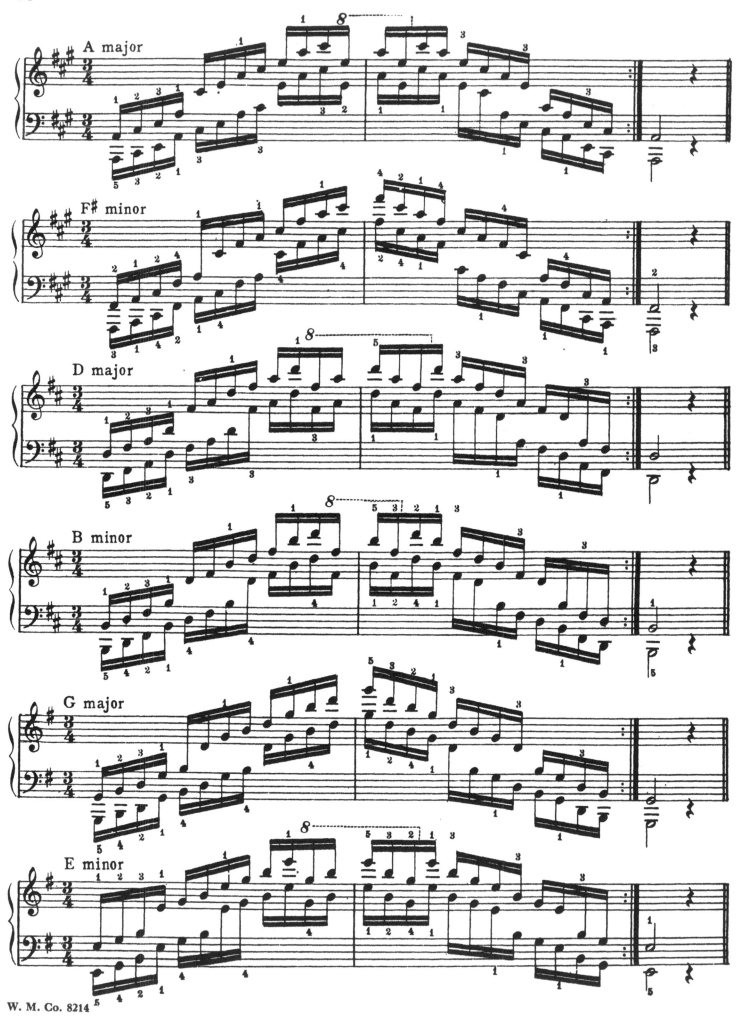

Extension of the fingers in chords
of the diminished seventh, in arpeggios

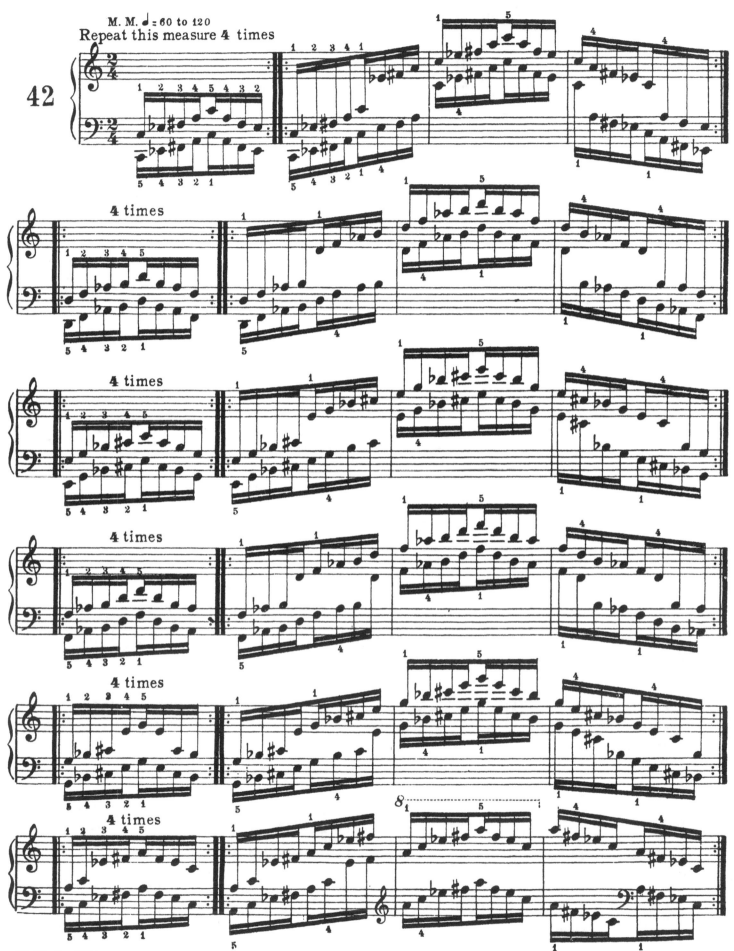

Extension of the fingers in chords
of the dominant seventh, in arpeggios

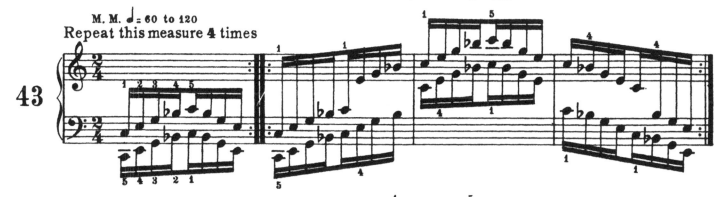

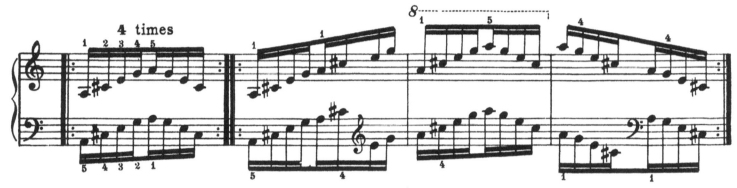

End of Part II

Parts I and II of this work being keys to the difficulties in Part III, it is most important that they should be throughly mastered before commencing the Virtuoso Studies contained in Part III.

W. M. Co. 8214

Part III

Virtuoso Exercises, for Obtaining a Mastery over the Greatest Mechanical Difficulties

Repeated notes in groups of three

Fingers lifted high and with precision, without raising hand or wrist. As the first four measures are well learned, take up the rest of the exercise.

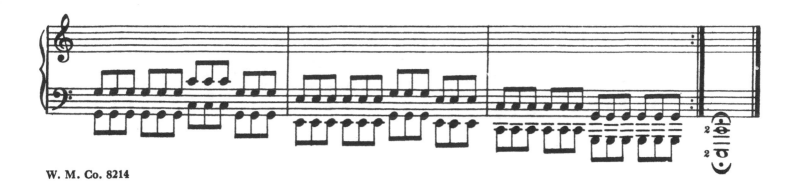

W. M. Co. 8214

Notes repeated in groups of two by all five fingers

Study the first fingering until throughly mastered; practise similarly each of the five follow-ing fingerings, then play through the exercise without stopping.

Accent the first of each pair of slurred notes

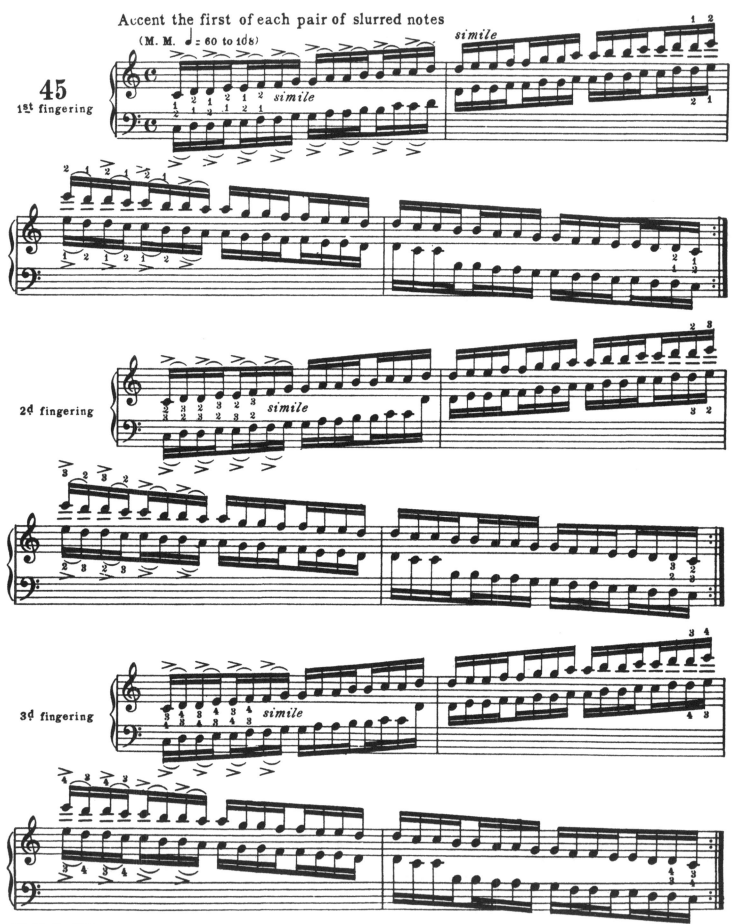

4th fingering

5th fingering

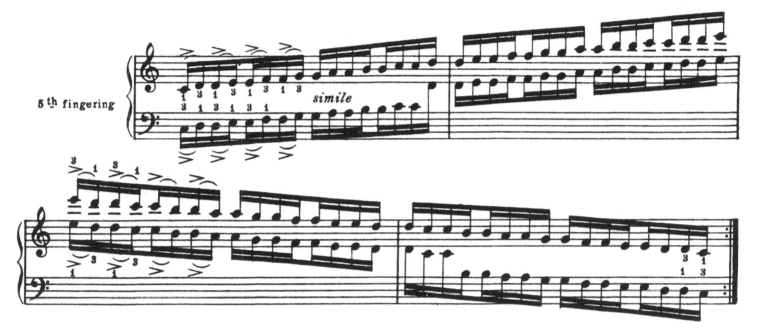

6th fingering

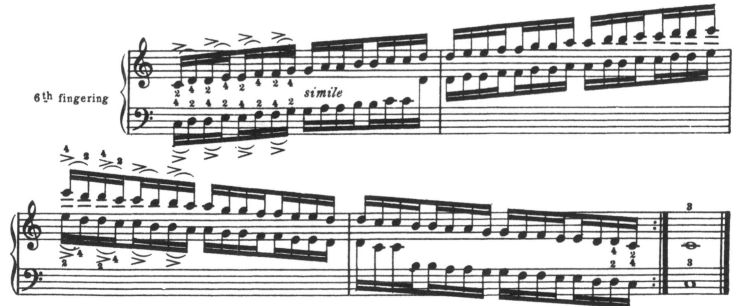

The Trill
for all five fingers.

Practise the first 6 measures until they can be executed in a rapid tempo; then practise the rest of the trill. Where the fingering is changed (1), be careful that not the slightest unevenness occurs.

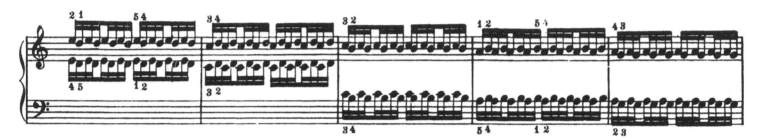

It is of interest to note that Mozart used this exercise for the study

of the trill

Thalberg's trill

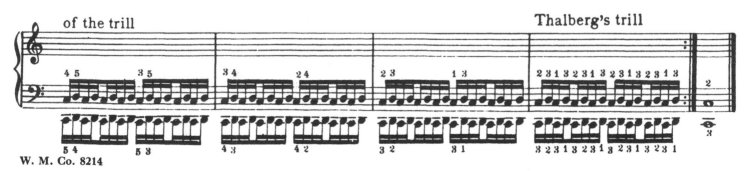

Notes repeated in groups of four

Fingers raised high and striking with precision throughout this exercise, without raising hand or wrist. When the first line is mastered, not before, take up the rest of the exercise.

Wrist-exercise
Detached Thirds and Sixths

Wrists well up after each stroke, holding the arms perfectly quiet; the wrist should be supple, and the fingers firm without stiffness. Practise the first four measures until an easy wrist-movement is obtained; then take up the rest of the exercise.

(M. M. ♩ = 40 to 84)

48

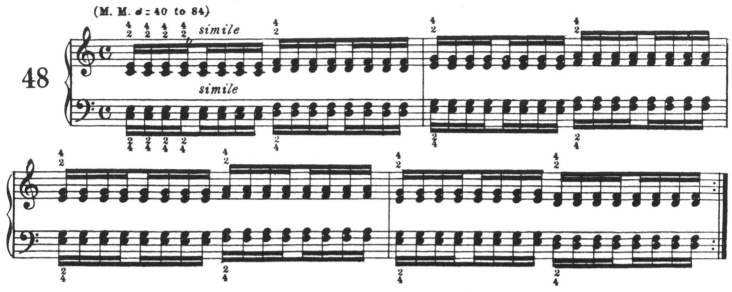

Detached Sixths

Same remarks as for the thirds
(M. M. ♩ = 40 to 84)

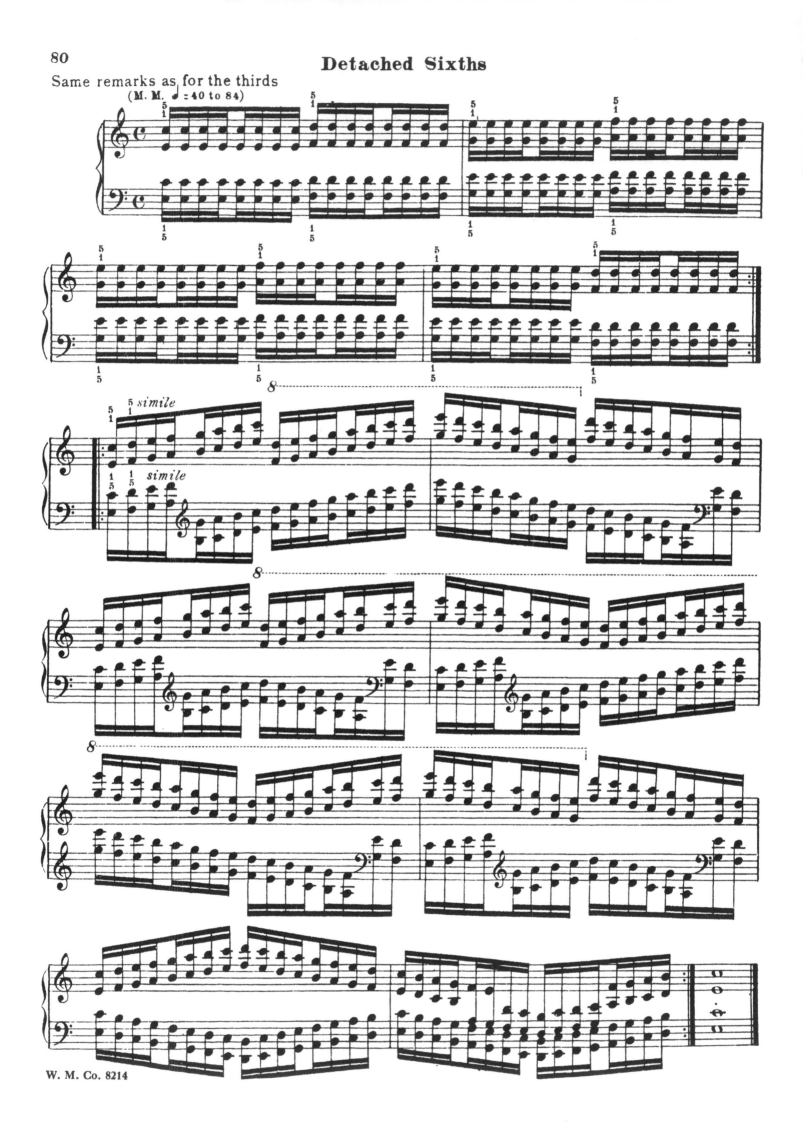

Stretches from the 1st to the 4th fingers, and from the 2d to the 5th, in each hand.

Very useful for increasing the stretching capacity of these fingers.

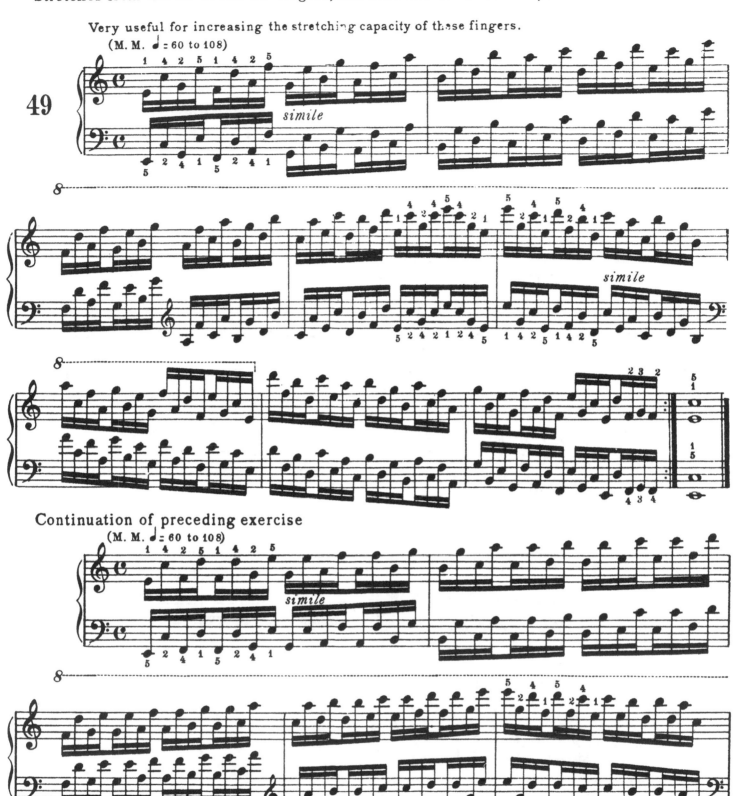

Continuation of preceding exercise

W. M. Co. 8214

Legato Thirds

Carefully study this exercise, as Thirds occupy a very important place in difficult music. All notes must be struck evenly and very distinctly.

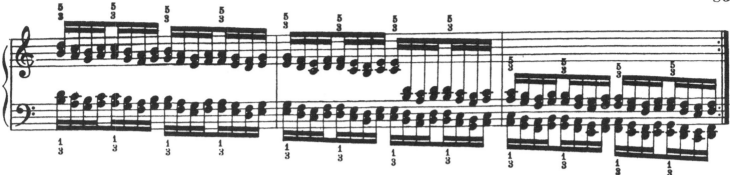

Scales in Legato Thirds

Scales in legato thirds must be practised to obtain a smooth legato. Keep the fifth finger of the right hand for an instant on its note while the thumb and 3d finger are passing over to the next third; in the left hand, the thumb is similarly held for an instant. Notes to be held are indicated by half-notes.(1) Proceed similarly in the chromatic scale further on, and in all scales in Thirds.

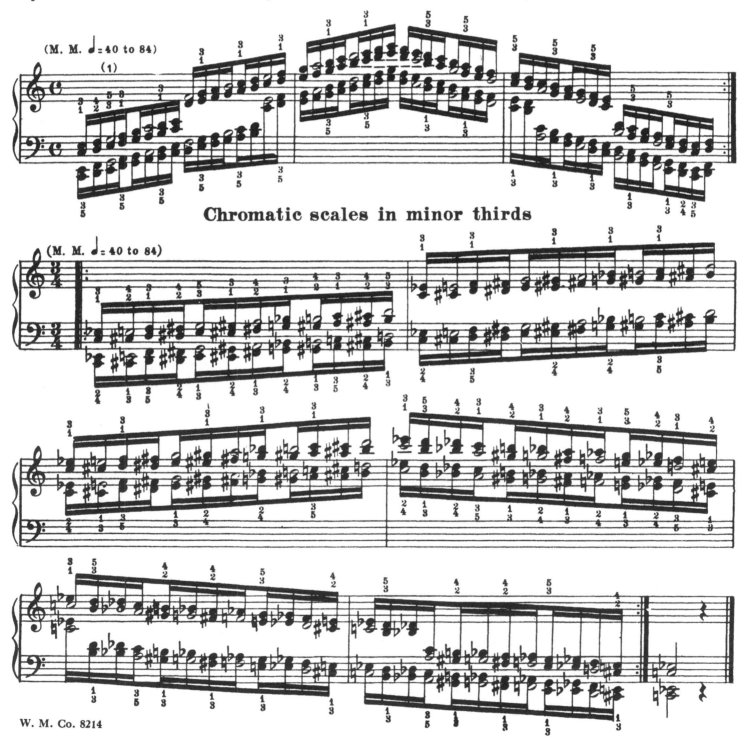

Chromatic scales in minor thirds

Preparatory Exercise for Scales in Octaves

The wrist should be very supple, the fingers taking the octaves should be held firmly but without stiffness and the other fingers should assume a slightly rounded position.

Repeat these three first lines slowly until a good wrist-movement is attained, and then accelerate the tempo, continuing without interruption. If the wrists become fatigued, play slowly until fatigue has disappeared, and then gradually accelerate up to tempo.

See remarks to № 48

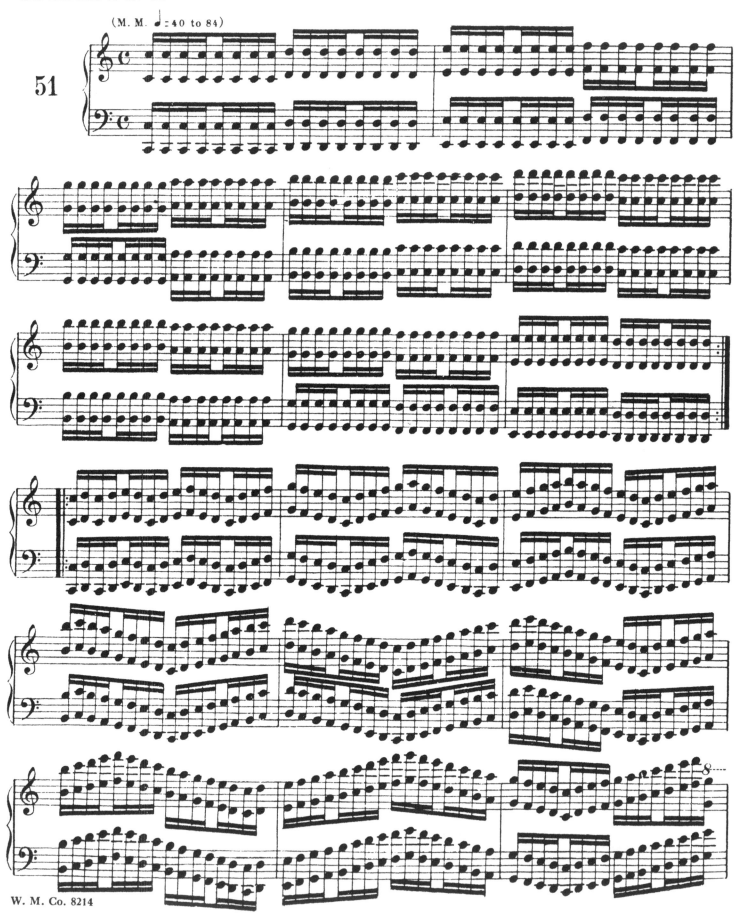

W. M. Co. 8214

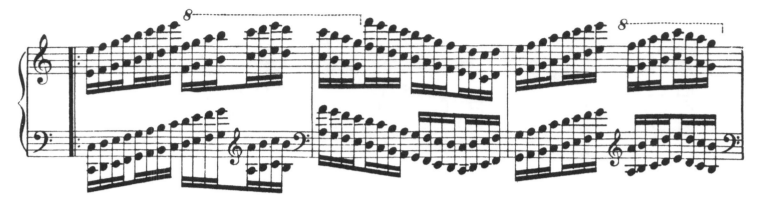

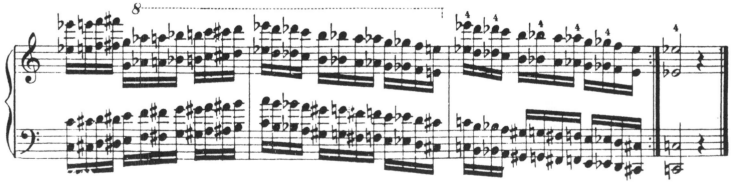

Scales in Thirds in the Keys Most Used

Play these scales legato, and very evenly; it is most important to master them thoroughly.

See remarks to N? 50

W. M. Co. 8214

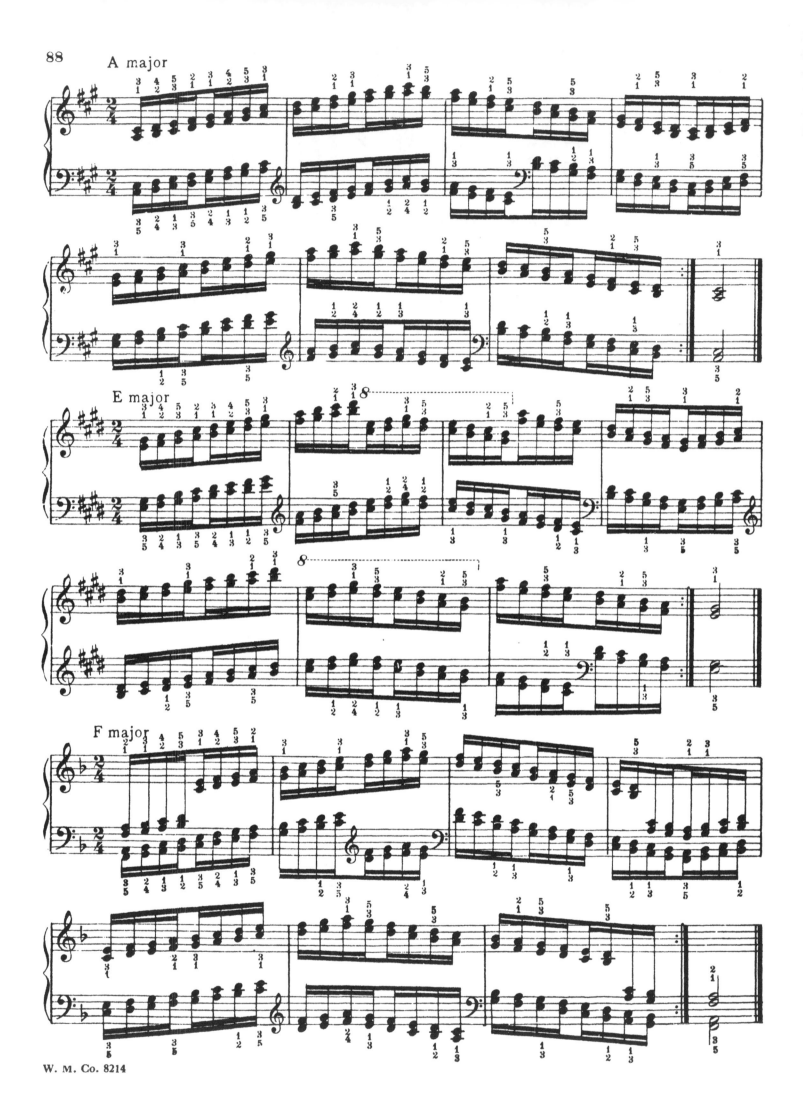

A major

E major

F major

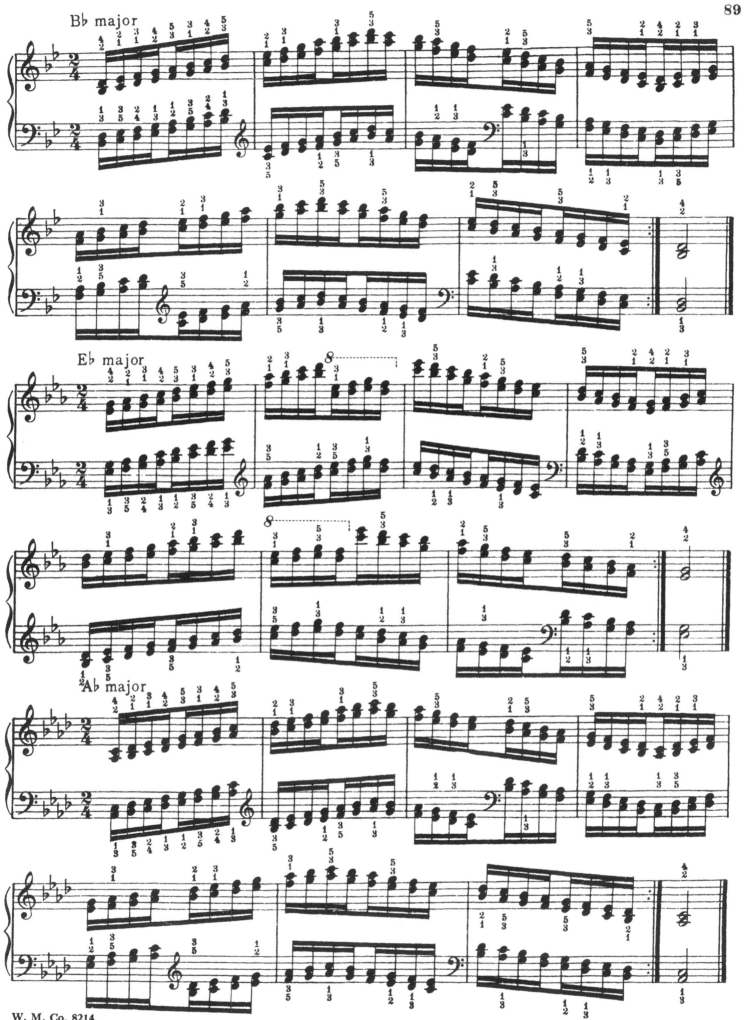

A minor

D minor

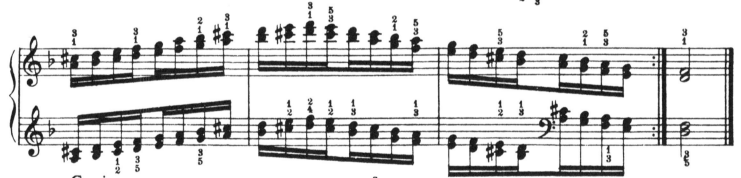

G minor

First practise each of these scales until it can be executed with facility then play through all 24 without interruption.

We cannot too strongly insist on the absolute necessity of a proper wrist movement; it is the only means of executing octaves without stiffness and with suppleness, vivacity and energy.

See the explanations for Nos 48 and 51

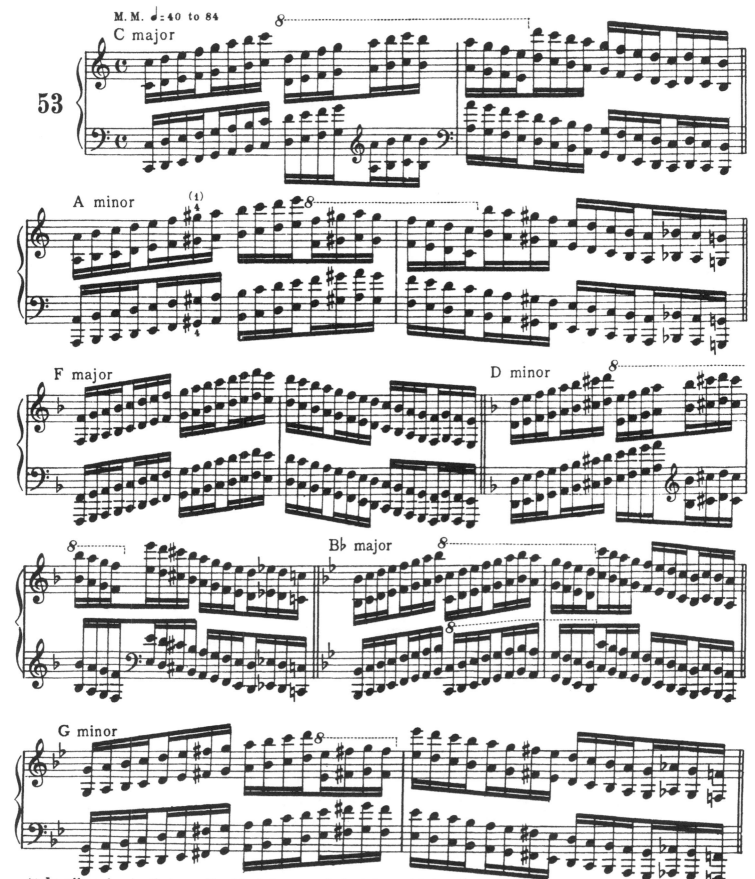

(1) In all scales in Octaves, the black keys are to be taken with the 4th finger of each hand.

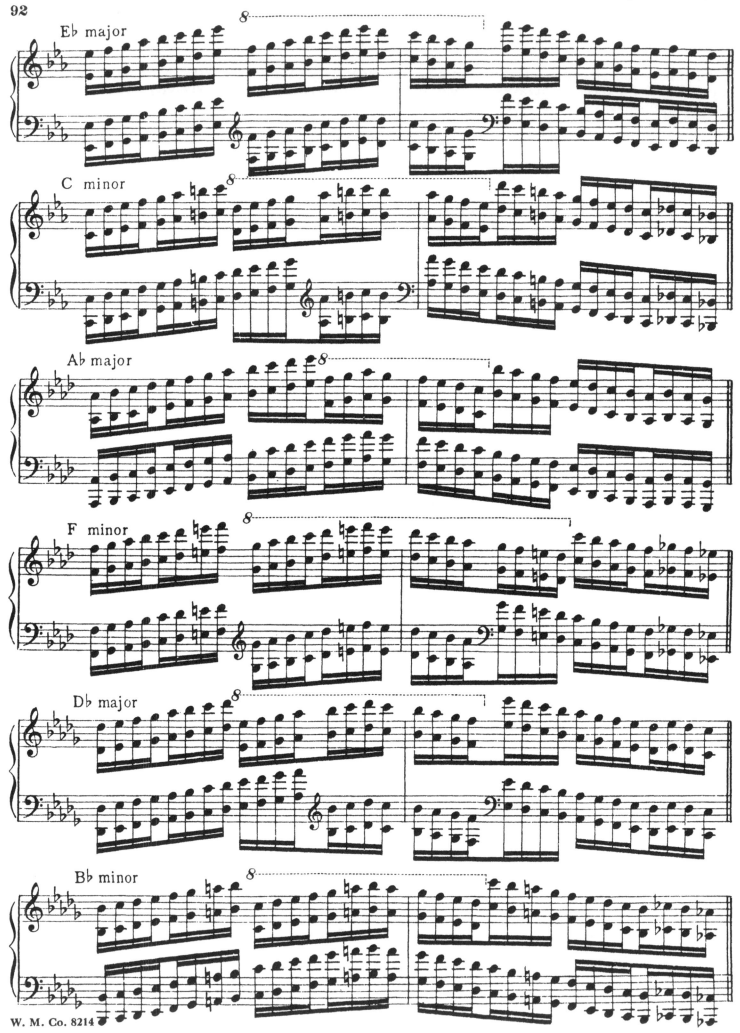

Gb major

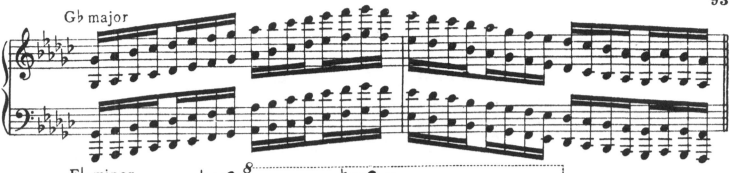

Eb minor

B major

G# minor

E major

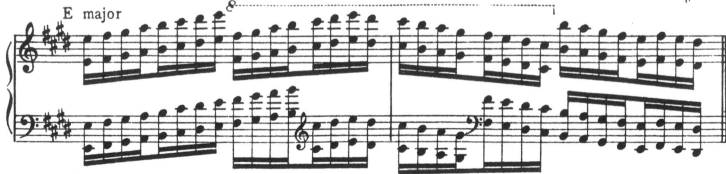

C# minor

A major

F# minor

D major

B minor

G major

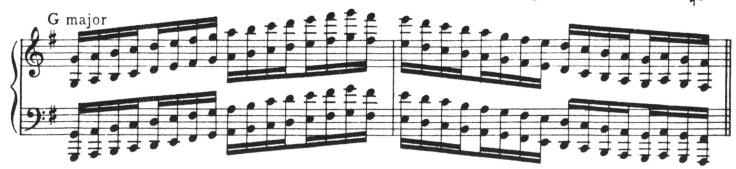

E minor

The Quadruple Trill in Thirds, for all five fingers

Execute this very smoothly and evenly. Each Third very clearly.

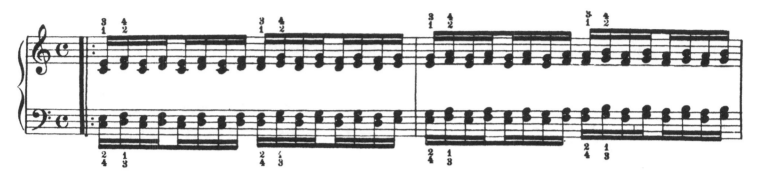

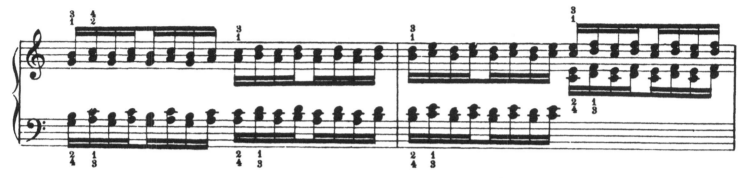

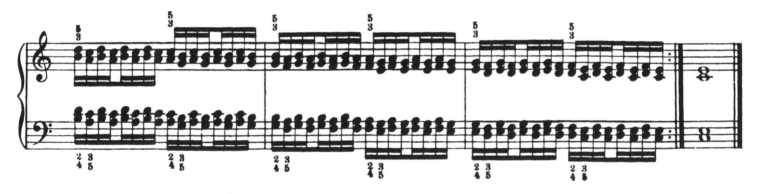

The Triple Trill

Same remark as for № **54**

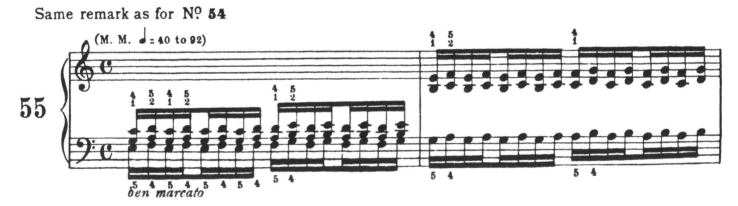

ben marcato

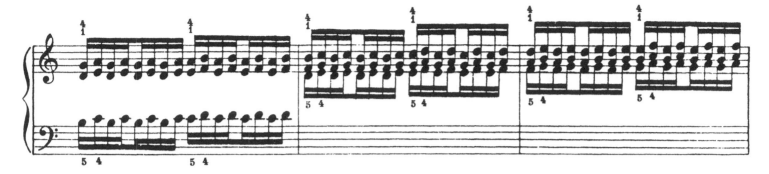

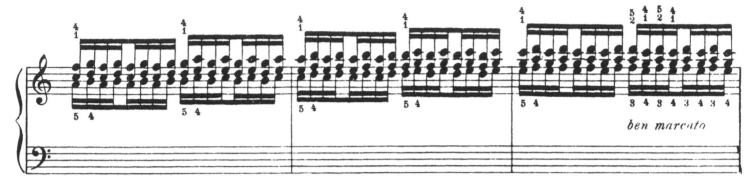

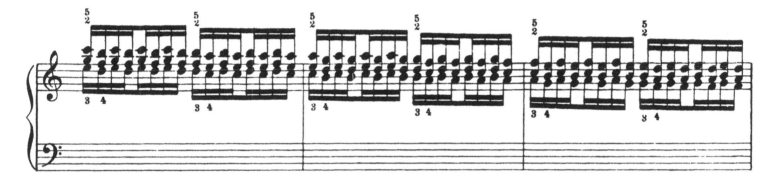

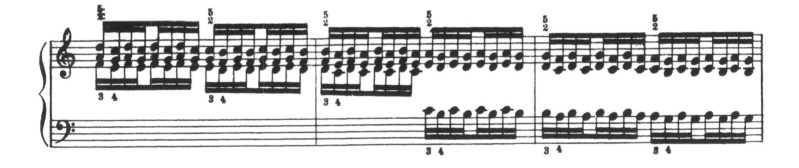

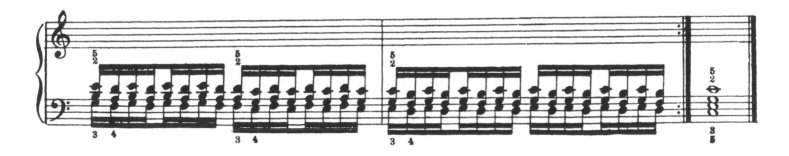

Special fingerings for the Quadruple Trill

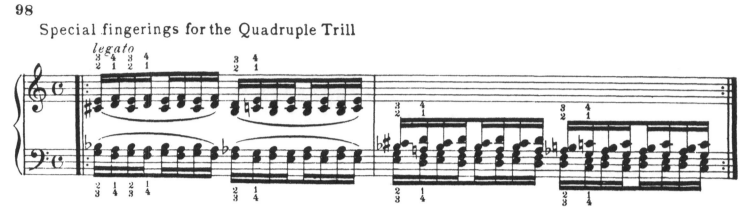

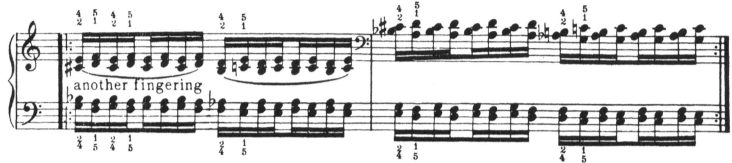

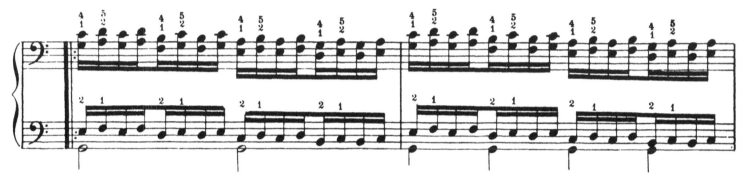

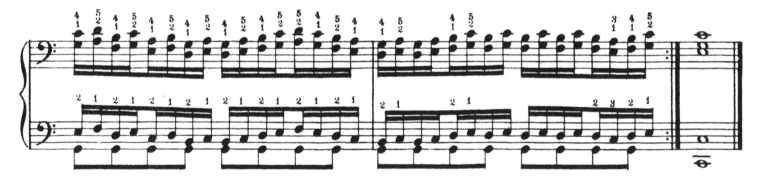

Scales in Broken Octaves in the 24 Keys

Play them through without stopping.
This highly important exercise likewise prepares the wrists for the study of the tremolo.

A minor

F major

D minor

Bb major

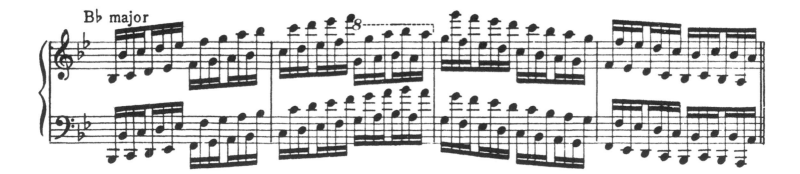

G minor

(1) Throughout this exercise, take the black keys with the 4th finger of each hand.

Eb major

C minor

Ab major

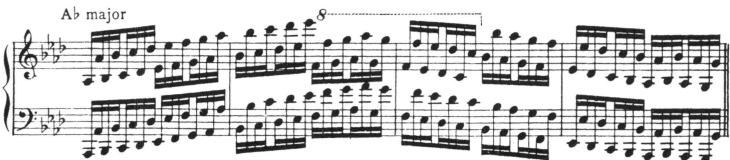

F minor

Db major

Bb minor

Gb major

Eb minor

B major

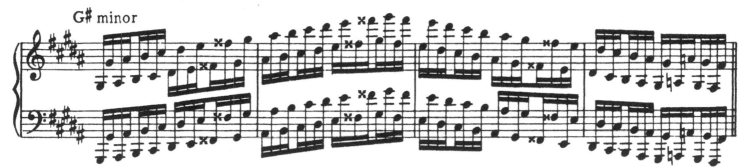

G# minor

F major

C# minor

A major

F# minor

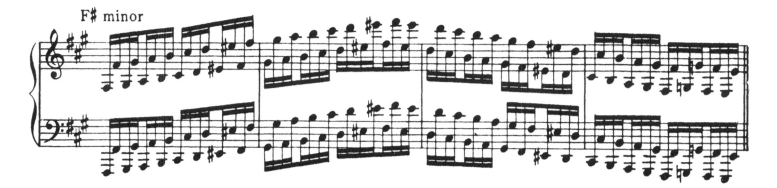

D major

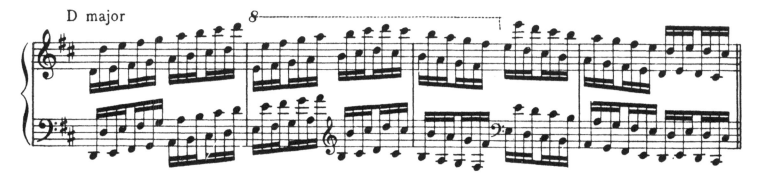

B minor

G major

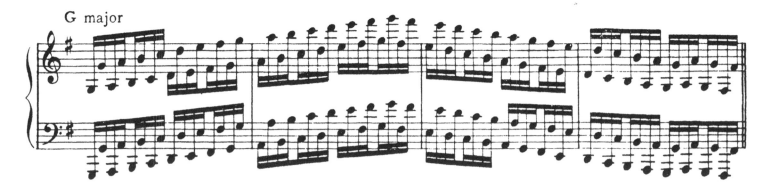

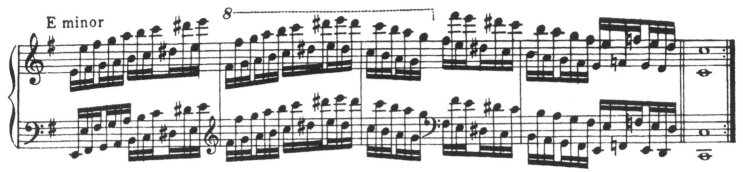

E minor

Broken Arpeggios in Octaves in the 24 Keys

Practise the first arpeggio in C, which must be played cleanly and distinctly, with a good wrist-movement.

Similarly practise each of the 24 arpeggios; then play them all through without interruption.

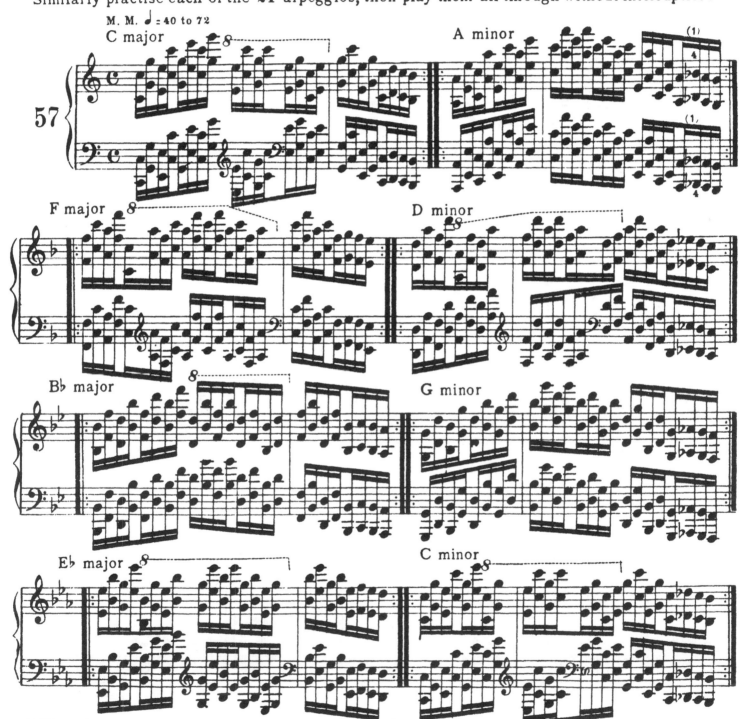

M. M. ♩ = 40 to 72

C major   A minor

57

F major   D minor

B♭ major   G minor

E♭ major   C minor

(1) Throughout this exercise, take the black keys with the 4th finger of each hand.

W. M. Co. 8214

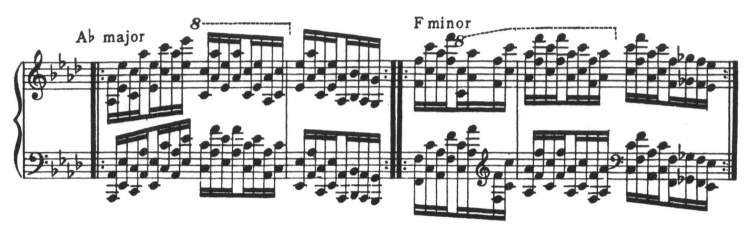

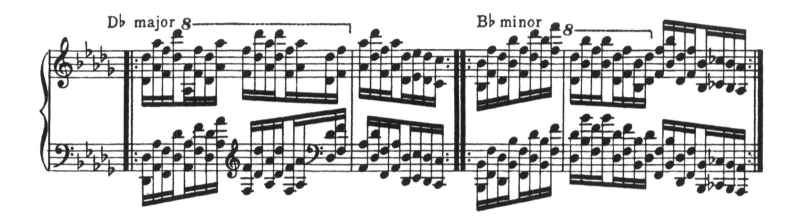

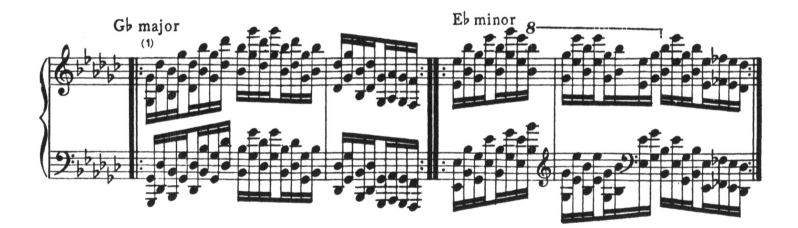

(1) As this arpeggio, and the next one in E♭ minor, are on black keys alone, either the 4th or 5th finger may be employed.

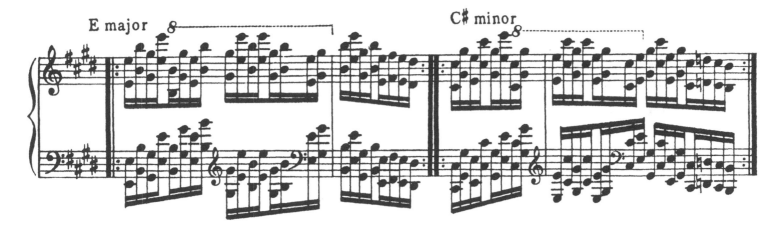

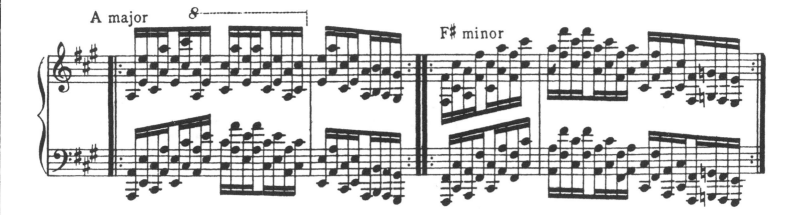

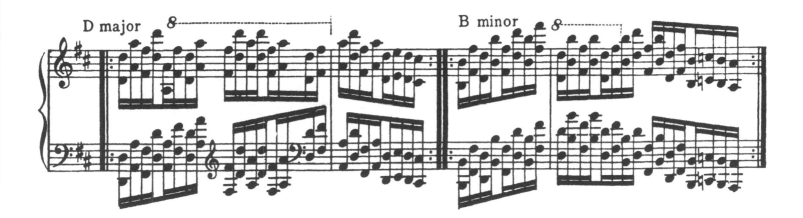

Sustained Octaves

Accompanied by detached notes

Strike the octaves vigorously without lifting the wrists, and hold them down while deftly exe -
cuting the intermediate notes with a good finger-action.

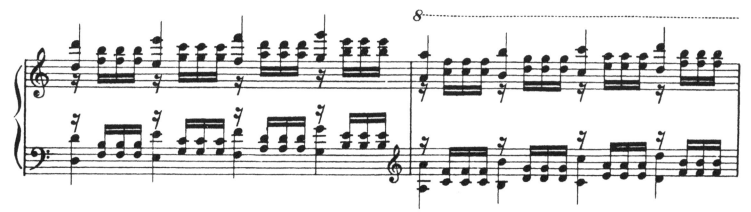

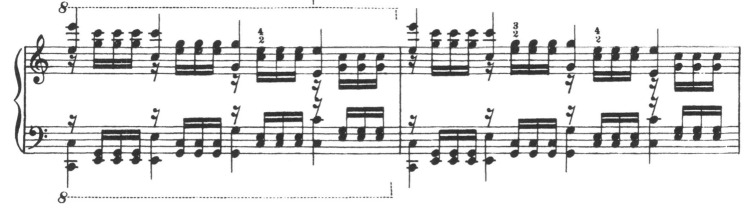

W. M. Co. 8214

Quadruple Trill in Sixths

for the combination of the 1st and 4th, and 2d and 5th, fingers of each hand.

Neither hand nor wrist should be moved in the least while playing this exercise.

59

Repeat this measure 4 times

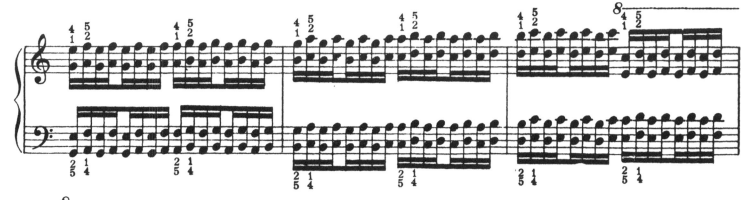

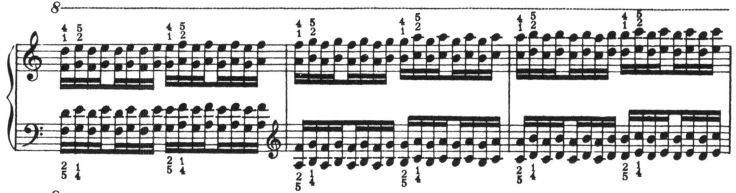

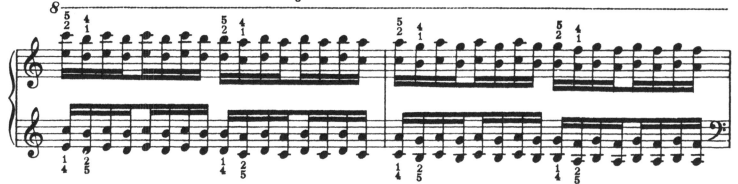

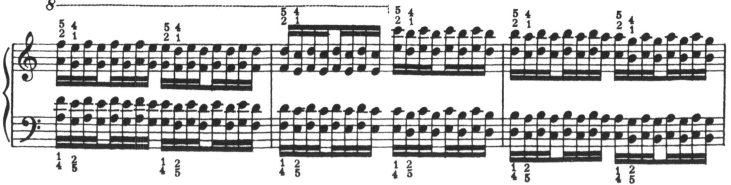

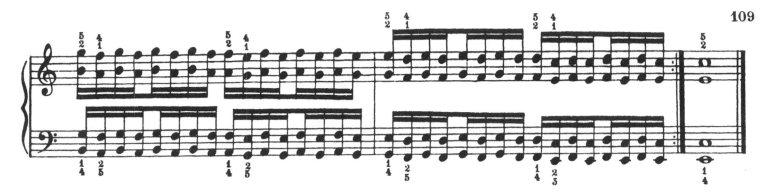

(M. M. ♩ = 40 to 84) *simile*

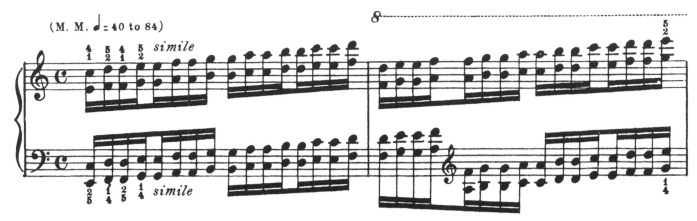

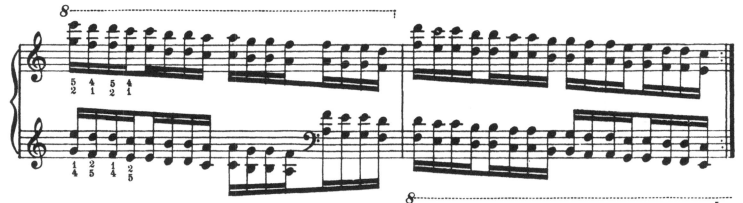

The Tremolo

To properly execute the tremolo, it should be played with the same rapidity as the roll on the drum.

Practise slowly at first; then gradually accelerate the tempo until the movement indicated (M. M. ♩=72) is reached. Finally, by oscillations of the wrists, the rapidity is still further augmented up to the tempo of the drum roll. This étude is long and difficult; but the result will repay the pianist for the trouble and fatigue. Steibelt made his hearers shiver by his execution of the tremolo.

60

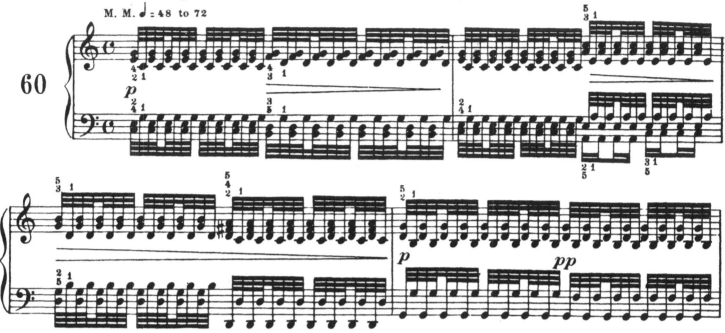

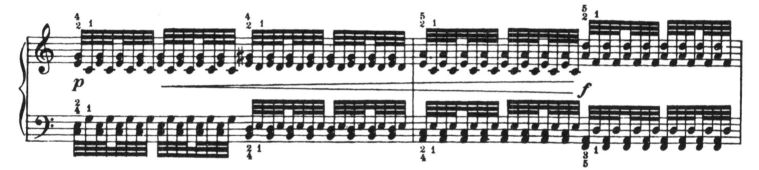

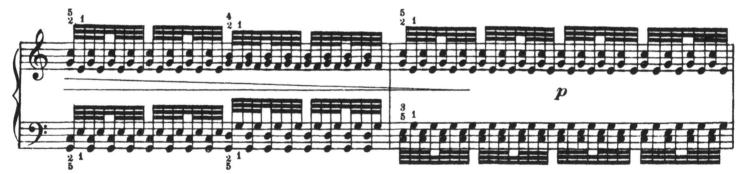

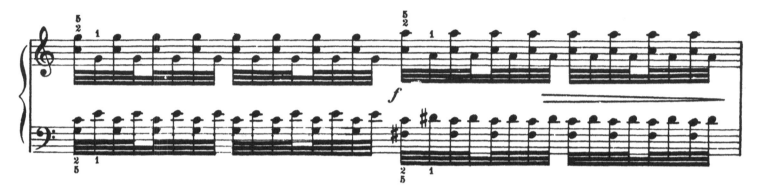

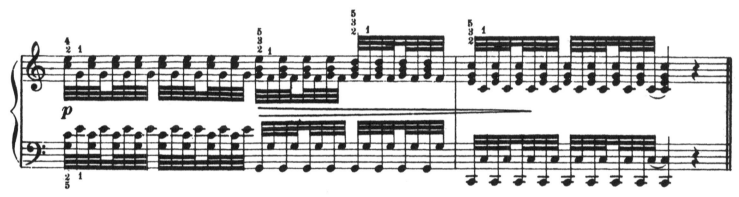

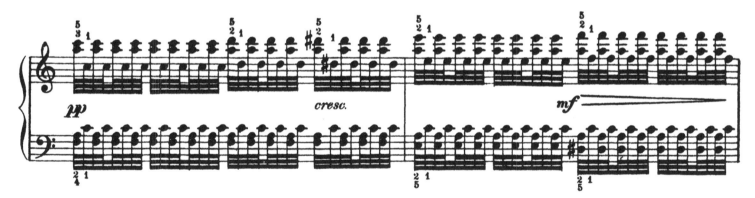

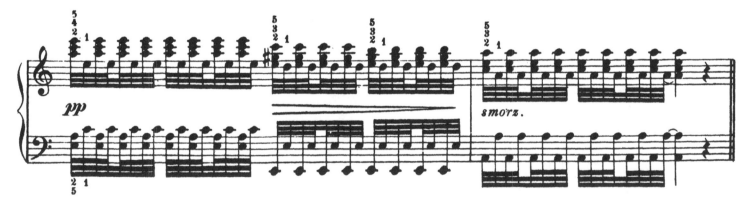

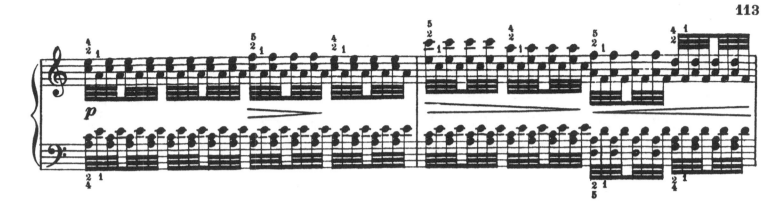

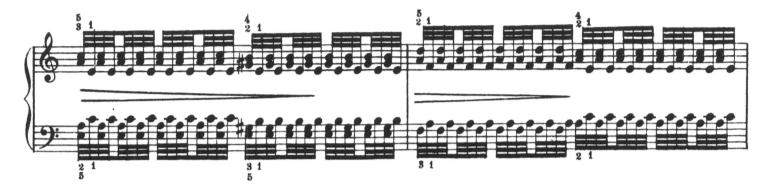

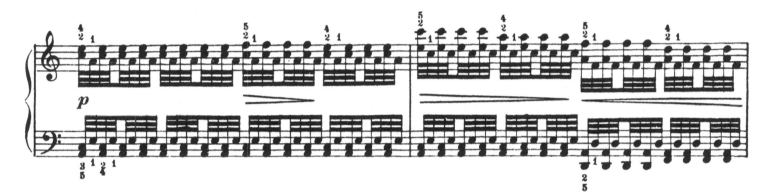

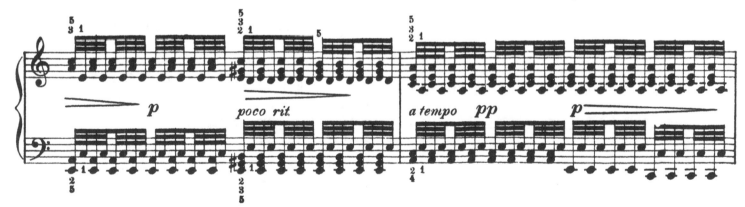

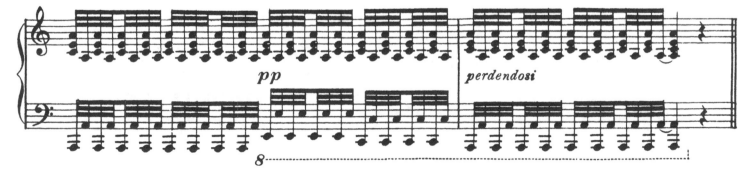

W. M. Co. 8214

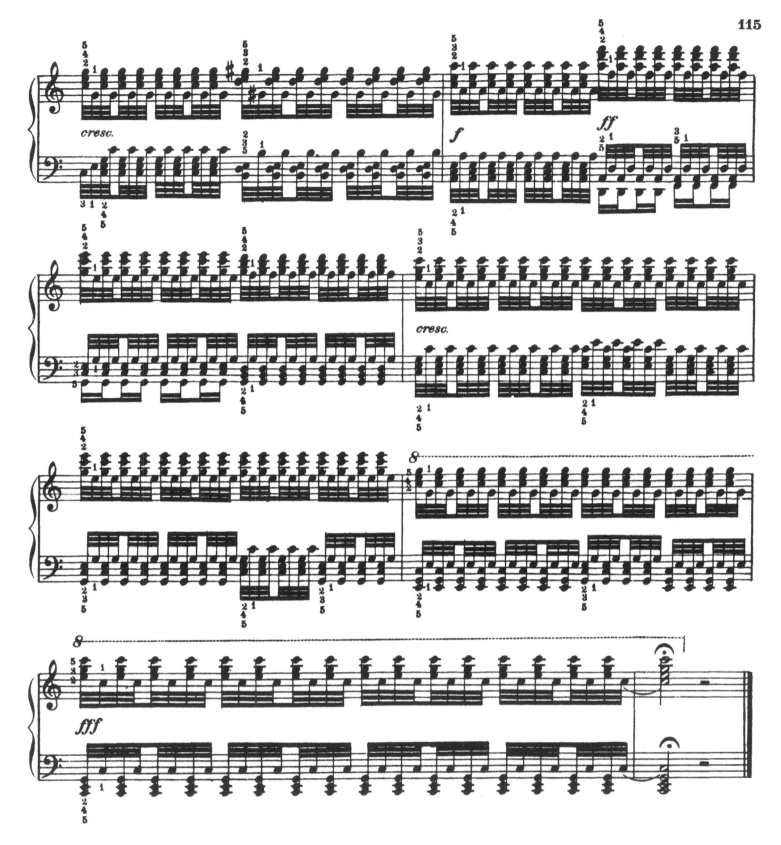

Now that the student has studied this volume, he is acquainted with the chief mechanical difficulties. But if he would enjoy the fruit of his toil, and become a real virtuoso, he should play this entire book every day for a considerable time. Only in this way can he familiarize himself with these great difficulties.

The greatest artists find it necessary to repeat daily exercises for several hours, merely to "keep up their playing." We should not, therefore, be accused of exaggerating the matter when we require of a student that he should play these exercises through every day.

The Willis Appreciation Series

WORKS OF THE MASTERS! Prefaced and annotated with a FULL PAGE
biography of the Composer with highlights and details of his works.

BACH

BOURREE IN C AND BOURREE IN C MINOR (from the third 'cello Suite). by Agnes Zimmermann . . . .
FANTASIA IN C MINOR . . . . .
GAVOTTE IN B MINOR — Originally Bourree (from the second sonata for violin). Trans. by Saint-Saens . . .
GIGUE IN B MINOR (from the third French Suite) . . . . .
GIGUE IN B FLAT (from the First Partita) . . . . .
JESU, JOY OF MAN'S DESIRING (Chorale from Cantata No. 147). by Sister M. Elaine, C.D.P. . . . . .
PRELUDE IN C (No. 1, from Well-Tempered Clavichord) . . . . .

BEETHOVEN

ALBUMBLATT (Fur Elise) . . . . .
ADIEU TO THE PIANO . . . . .
BAGATELLE IN E FLAT. Op. 33, No. 1 . . . . .
MINUET IN G . . . . .
RONDO IN C MAJOR. Op. 51, No. 1 . . . . .
SONATINA IN G MAJOR . . . . .
SONATINA IN F . . . . .

BRAHMS

HUNGARIAN DANCE No. 5 . . . . .
RHAPSODY. Op. 79, No. 2 . . . . .

CHOPIN

ETUDE IN C MINOR (The Revolutionary). Op. 10, No 12 . . . . .
ETUDE IN E MAJOR . . . . .
ETUDE. Op. 25, No. 9 G♭ Major . . . . .
FANTAISE (Impromptu). Op. 66 . . . . .
MAZURKA IN B FLAT. Op. 7, No. 1 . . . . .
MINUTE WALTZ. Op. 64, No. 1 . . . . .
NOCTURNE IN E FLAT. Op. 9, No. 2 . . . . .
POLONAISE IN A MAJOR. Op. 40, No. 1 . . . . .
POLONAISE IN C SHARP MINOR. Op. 26, No. 1 . . . . .
VALSE BRILLANTE IN A♭. Op. 34, No. 1 . . . . .
VALSE IN D FLAT. Op. 64, No. 1 . . . . .
VALSE IN C SHARP MINOR. Op. 64, No. 2 . . . . .

GRIEG

BIRDLING. Op. 43, No. 4 . . . . .
BUTTERFLY. Op. 43, No. 1 . . . . .
DANCE CAPRICE. Op. 28, No. 3 . . . . .
ELFIN DANSE. Op. 12, No. 4 . . . . .
I LOVE THEE . . . . .
MARCH OF THE DWARFS. Op. 54, No. 3 . . . . .
NOCTURNE. Op. 54, No. 4 . . . . .
TO THE SPRING. Op. 43, No. 6 . . . . .

SCHUBERT

HARK HARK! THE LARK! (Transcription by Liszt) . . . . .
IMPROMPTU. Op. 90, No. 4 . . . . .
MINUETTO. Op. 78 . . . . .
MILITARY MARCH. Op. 51, No. 1 . . . . .
SCHERZO . . . . .
THREE WALTZES. Op. 98 . . . . .
THE TROUT (Heller) . . . . .

THE WILLIS MUSIC COMPANY